brilliant

answers
to tough
interview
questions

answers
to tough
interview
questions

fourth edition

Susan Hodgson

Prentice Hall
is an imprint of

Harlow, England • London • New York • Boston • San Francisco • Toronto • Sydney • Singapore • Hong Kong
Tokyo • Seoul • Taipei • New Delhi • Cape Town • Madrid • Mexico City • Amsterdam • Munich • Paris • Milan

PEARSON EDUCATION LIMITED

Edinburgh Gate
Harlow CM20 2JE
Tel: +44 (0)1279 623623
Fax: +44 (0)1279 431059
Website: www.pearsoned.co.uk

First published in Great Britain in 2002
Second edition published 2005
Third edition published 2008
Fourth edition published 2011

© Pearson Education 2002, 2011

The right of Susan Hodgson to be identified as author of this work has been asserted by her in accordance with the Copyright, Designs and Patents Act 1988.

Pearson Education is not responsible for the content of third party internet sites.

ISBN: 978-0-273-74389-7

British Library Cataloguing-in-Publication Data
A catalogue record for this book is available from the British Library

Library of Congress Cataloging-in-Publication Data
Hodgson, Susan.
    Brilliant answers to tough interview questions / Susan Hodgson. -- 4th ed.
        p. cm.
    Includes index.
    ISBN 978-0-273-74389-7 (pbk.)
    1. Employment interviewing--Handbooks, manuals, etc. 2. Applications for
positions--Examinations, questions, etc. 3. Self-presentation. 4. Interpersonal
communication. I. Title. II. Title: Answers to tough interview questions.
    HF5549.5.I6H58 2011
    650.14'4--dc22
                          2010040870

10 9 8 7 6 5 4 3
14 13 12

Typeset in 10/14pt Plantin Regular by 3
Printed and bound in Malaysia (CTP-PJB)

Contents

About the author

Susan Hodgson was head of the Careers Service at London South Bank University in London. There she taught job-hunting skills to students and trained them in interview techniques. She worked with a wide range of employers to ensure that she knew exactly what they were looking for. She has worked with school leavers, university students and professional people seeking a change of career.

Susan Hodgson writes on many careers and employment topics – writing articles, website material and books. She currently works as a career consultant and freelance writer, and is based in Dorset.

Acknowledgements

Thanks go to Andrew Chapman, John Dean, Robert Fox, Diane Goff, Geoff Hodgson, Margaret Holbrough, Jo Horne, Andrew Perrins and Joan Sanders.

Introduction

Setting the scene

Sitting in a dentist's waiting room, taking your driving test, turning over an examination paper, getting out of a mobile phone shop without a new contract or attending a job interview are familiar experiences to most people. They also trigger predictable reactions for most of us – a sense of trepidation and a longing for them to be over and done with and for life to return to normal. In one case at least, that of being called to a selection interview, there is a great deal that you can do to alleviate this sense of anxiety and to turn the situation around to one that, if not actually *looking forward* to, you at least feel thoroughly equal to dealing with.

brilliant tip

Start by realising you have just received excellent news. You have been asked to the interview because your CV, your application form or your telephone call has struck the right note – you have whetted somebody's appetite and they believe you could be the person they are looking for.

The world of selection interviewing is not the TV world of *The Apprentice* or *Dragons' Den*. It is not inhabited by sadists who spend their days planning ways of making candidates feel inadequate and stupid (at least, not in most cases). It is peopled by hard-pressed managers, supervisors and human resources staff who desperately want to make the right decision for their organisations. They do not want to cost their companies time and money while a post is re-advertised, a new short list drawn up and a training programme started all over again because they had inflicted a quiet and moody loner on their busy sales team or recruited a flamboyant socialite to work as the manager of a silent retreat. Put like this, they may not actually win your sympathy and understanding but you may gain a new perspective, one from which you can really benefit. Help them by being a well-prepared, good interviewee and help yourself to give a really convincing performance. Even if, on some occasions, you don't get the job, you should come away feeling you have given a really good account of yourself, and learn to do even better next time.

Recruiters take selection equally seriously whether economic times are good or bad. Don't be tempted into an attitude that interviews won't count for much if there are not so many jobs around, because the employers can simply interview more candidates. It does not work like that.

brilliant tip

Help them by being a well-prepared, good interviewee and help yourself to give a really convincing performance.

That is not to say that interviews are easy – they are not. They are demanding and stressful, and, even if they sometimes seem low key, you are still being put on the spot and given this one opportunity to get something that you really want. Knowing what you are up against and what you can do about it is the essential psychological and tactical starting point for anyone who has been invited to a job interview. This may happen when:

- you are applying for your first job after leaving school;
- you have just completed a course at university or college;
- you are in the process of changing your career direction either through choice or as a result of market forces;
- you are making a sideways move in your field of employment;
- you are returning to work after a period of absence raising children or caring for other family members; or
- you are seeking promotion in your present profession.

Regardless of what kind of work you are applying for – full-time, part-time, professional, practical, technical, administrative, creative or caring – you will have to convince a person or a panel of people that you are the ideal choice. To add to your difficulties, every other candidate will be trying to do exactly the same thing.

brilliant tip

Daunting and stressful as interviews may be, they also provide a golden opportunity for you to take centre stage – make the most of it.

Take care not to take the references to acting too literally though. Showing the most confident and convincing side of yourself works well, but be careful not to create a false persona that is nothing like the real you. This puts a strain on you, and the interviewer can almost always tell that you are not relaxed and natural. If you have to pretend to be someone you are not, you probably wouldn't enjoy the job anyway.

It is easy to neglect interview preparation as part of your job-hunting strategy. Preparing a really good CV and ensuring that you fill in application forms really well, combined with all your research on whom to apply to and when to apply can mean that interview preparation ends up taking a back seat. Many people say that it is the paper part of the application process that they really hate and that if only they can get to an interview and talk to employers face to face they will be fine. As the invitation to an interview drops on to the doormat, or materialises in the e-mail in-box, breezy optimism flies out of the window. Talking to employers face to face isn't quite so easy. What questions will they ask and what answers will you be able to give?

This book will help *anyone* who has been invited to *any* kind of selection interview for *any* job to prepare more effectively, feel more confident and be well armed to deal with whatever questions – obvious, tricky or challenging – are thrown at them.

The chapters that follow will guide you through all the most commonly asked interview questions. You will find questions about you, your experience, your education, your competences, your interests, your ambitions and your personality, as well as questions about your choice of job and why you are applying to a particular company or organisation.

Questions without answers do nothing to relieve your anxiety, so each chapter offers examples of model answers that are likely to hit the right spot with employers. A model answer is fine, but it is just that, a model. It cannot cover every single set of circumstances that occur in every individual's job search and career development. For many of the questions, you will find that more than one suggested answer is given to illustrate how these answers have to be tailored to specific circumstances. For the first question in each chapter, the model answer is analysed in a little more detail to show you some of the elements that go into making up a good response. This will help you to construct your own answers.

Interview questions and answers are not mathematical formulae; there is never only one 'right' answer. This book also provides tips and exercises that will help you make the connection between the model answers set out and those answers that you would really feel happy to use and which describe your own circumstances.

Chapter 6, for example, on exploring your career choice, cannot outline every possible answer justifying choices of everything from accountant to zookeeper, but it can enable you to focus on what questions you are likely to be asked concerning why you have chosen a particular job or profession and give you guidelines on developing suitable answers.

This book will be useful right across the employment spectrum. It is not designed only for those who are pursuing jobs in the commercial and business sector, but will provide advice suitable for you whether you work in education, healthcare, commerce, industry, manufacturing or the media. In many chapters, you will find the use of the word 'company' referring to potential employers, but this is really shorthand for any employing organisation with which you may be seeking employment.

brilliant tip

For your answers to be really effective, don't use the model answers like a script to be learned. If you try to use them in this way they will sound false; the answer won't apply to you 100 per cent and trying to memorise material will only generate additional pre-interview stress. Use your skills and knowledge to adapt the answers so they work well for you.

This flexible attitude to constructing your answers also applies to the way you consider the wording of questions. Always think about what a questioner is really getting at when they ask you a question. This book phrases questions in the way they are most likely to arise in job interviews and it also asks some very similar questions using different forms of wording to help you become more familiar with common interview language. Interviewers are human (even if there are some occasions when you have cause to doubt this) and they will have their own particular styles of questioning. 'What are you good at?' 'What are your strengths?' 'What makes you stand out from the crowd?' These are all questions that are asking you to distinguish your main selling points – to demonstrate your assets.

When you attend interviews, don't be surprised if the language both you and your questioner use is less formal than that used in the examples in this book. Human nature is more idiosyncratic, more varied and more individual than any invented questioners and candidates. Naturally, there is a difference between a real conversation, where you and the interviewer have hopefully begun to build up some rapport, and a situation where specific questions and answers are being illustrated out of context. As a rule, interviewees tend to reflect the general tone and language adopted by their interviewer – this happens automatically, so candidates don't have to agonise and worry over whether they will get this right. In real, 'live' interviews it is often quite acceptable to include an element of humour, without trying to do a one-person stand-up comedy show for half an hour. Humour is highly individual and candidates should follow their intuition and gut feelings about when to use it – it is not something that can be prepared for in advance.

When using the model questions and answers, you will find it is often quite clear as to the kind of information the interviewer requires, so you won't find explanatory notes before or after every question and answer. Where, however, there is some doubt, or where additional pointers may be helpful, these are included, along with tips to help you focus on your own potential answers.

To ensure you can adapt the answers to your own circumstances, many chapters contain brief questionnaires that help you focus on your past, your future, your strengths, your achievements, your values and your interests – all those things that matter to you and, when you are applying for jobs, matter to your future employer. These are not scored questionnaires that offer an external interpretation of you; instead they act as prompts and thought generators for you and will help your interview preparation.

You will find help in the following chapters to fit your particular circumstances, whether you have just left school or university, are seeking a change in career direction, returning to work after a break of some kind, or seeking an important promotion. The chapters are organised to highlight particular aspects of experience, education, employment history, interests, motivation and achievements, personality, ambitions and career choice and development.

Inevitably, because you are being given ideal models to work from in the answers, you may find the model 'applicants' seem irritatingly close to perfection because they are composites of useful experiences and personal qualities. Do not be daunted by these paragons of selection-process perfection. Sample questions and answers include examples of applicants who might not always have been successful and have not always trodden a straight path to career success. The key to all their answers and to all those that you develop for yourself is drawing the positive out of the normal – the convincing out of the average and the extraordinary out of the ordinary.

brilliant tip

You can raise your confidence by becoming so familiar with any likely areas of questioning at an interview that you are unlikely to be caught unawares. You will be able to work out what the interviewer is really after even if the questions arise in different forms and, most importantly of all, you will know what it is you have to offer and what you want to get across in order to maximise your chance of securing the position you desire.

All the questions and answers are based on what interview candidates state they find difficult and what employers say they are really looking for.

A final word of encouragement – understand that performing well at interviews is a skill at which you really can improve and good preparation will undoubtedly accelerate this improvement.

CHAPTER 1

The point of preparation – the art of preparation

How to be brilliantly prepared for the interview and how to impress and sparkle on the day

That much quoted phrase 'Be prepared' is far more than a tired cliché when you receive an invitation to an interview. The following are key to making a powerful impact at any interview:

- researching appropriate information;
- preparing yourself mentally;
- anticipating the questions you are likely to be asked; and
- working out the best possible answers to these questions.

This book is all about considering the questions you could be asked and preparing concise, effective, persuasive answers that will help you to stand out from the crowd. As an interviewee, you will have to prepare to answer questions on every aspect of your education, employment history, ambitions and personal strengths. Since most interviews take between 25 and 40 minutes, you are unlikely to be quizzed on everything you have prepared, but you won't get caught out. Getting ready for an interview should not be like revising for an exam, where you realise you have revised the wrong topics. Neither does preparation for an interview involve learning possible answers parrot fashion. Good interview preparation means becoming so familiar with the points that you want to put across that you are able to listen to what is being asked and immediately bring forth the most convincing answers.

Remind yourself that almost all the questions you will be asked are designed to find out more about you and, most important of all, your suitability for a particular position and the likelihood of your fitting in well with your colleagues, your managers, your customers, your clients, your company, its staff and its work style. In general, all interviewers are seeking the answers to three fundamental questions.

Can you do the job? Do you have the appropriate mix of qualifications and/or experience to provide you with the basic skills and knowledge to do the job?

Will you do the job? This is quite a different question from 'can you' – this question is all about your willingness to do the work. Are you keen and eager; how can you demonstrate your motivation?

Will you fit in? This is all about your suitability to work in that particular set-up. Part of the answer to this question is hard to put into formal questions and answers; it is something you put over and the interviewer takes in at a more intuitive level. There are, however, whole sets of questions that do relate to this area – those questions about teamwork, dealing with difficult situations with other members of staff, being adaptable, flexible and friendly.

Given that the interviewer wants to know about you, make sure this is a topic with which you are happy, familiar and enthusiastic. You may have come to take yourself for granted by now, so take time to sit down and really think about what your qualities and your strengths are. Be aware of any weak spots that an interviewer may hone in on. Beware of doing yourself down. Many of us are far quicker at listing our drawbacks than our assets. Part of your preparation should be reminding yourself of your skills. The short questionnaire later in the chapter will help you to focus on your main selling points.

Of course different jobs require different portfolios of skills and experience, but there is a core of skills and attributes that feature in many job adverts and on many job descriptions, regardless of the position advertised. Your own observations, knowledge and/ or experience of the particular field of employment concerned will help you work out what combination of these skills is most important for the kind of work for which you are applying. A psychotherapist probably needs greater listening skills than a chartered accountant, for example, and the creativity of someone writing a catchy advertising slogan is not the same as the creativity of a food technologist developing a smoothie recipe.

Build your confidence

Increase your awareness of your own skills. Work through the questionnaire overleaf. Be honest, but err on the side of being generous to yourself.

Now look carefully at your list and where you rated yourself as good on a skill, then think of an occasion or situation when you have used this skill or quality to good effect.

brilliant tip

To ensure your skills and good qualities stand out and hit home you must be able to quote examples. Use examples from work situations, leisure and voluntary activities, your education or your home life.

Don't simply list skills without examples – all this does is irritate your interviewer and leave him or her unconvinced by what you are saying. It shows that you are good at reading adverts and job descriptions rather than that you are well qualified for the post.

Rate which of the following skills you possess. Be as honest as you can, but beware of being too hard on yourself.

Key

0 = You do not possess the skill

1 = You possess the skill to some degree

2 = You possess the skill to a high level of competence

Selling point	Score
Good with numbers	
Good at writing formal documents, reports, etc.	
Write good, clear e-mails and respond quickly to other e-mails	
Good creative writing skills (stories, poems, biography, etc.)	
Good at talking to people face to face	
Good at talking to people on the telephone, teleconferencing, etc.	
Good at taking decisions	
Good at listening to other people's problems	
Good at advising and helping people	
Good at persuading people to your point of view	
Good at solving intellectual problems	
Good at solving practical problems	
Good at organising your time and prioritising your workload	
Good at meeting deadlines	
Good at designing on paper, with your hands or with the aid of computers	
Good at building things to someone else's specifications	
Good level of IT literacy – knowledge of software/hardware	
Good specialist IT skills, e.g. Web design, graphics, interactive media	
Good at working flexibly within a team	

Selling point	Score
Good at taking responsibility for your own actions and your own work	
Able to work on your own without supervision	
Able to follow instructions given by others	
Able to delegate work to others	
Good at explaining things to other people, teaching skills to others	
Able to pay attention to detail	
Able to work under pressure	
Able to motivate other people	
Able to use your own initiative	
Able to think on your feet	
Able to learn tasks or assimilate information quickly	
Able to cope with changing circumstances	

brilliant tip

If you are lucky enough to have a detailed job description that sets out specific selection criteria or a person specification, ensure that you have relevant material to talk about against each criterion mentioned. Interviews based on these may require the interviewer to score candidates against each criterion, so don't miss any out.

This book returns often to the need to be really familiar with solid examples that highlight your skills. This is essential not just because the interviewer needs to know that you really do have this skill, but also because an interview is only a brief opportunity to show yourself in a brilliant light. If you can draw on a good range of examples and situations, you will make a good impression.

While research shows that interviews are actually rather an inaccurate selection tool – past performance and aptitude tests are probably a better guide – they are still central to any job selection. Don't take them lightly and do put in time on planning.

brilliant tip

If you know what you can offer and you can put it across effectively, you are well on the way to giving a brilliant interview performance and making a great impression.

Giving brilliant answers

Of course, the content of what you say is very important, but there are a few basic rules that will help all your answers to make the best possible impression.

The style of questions is an important consideration. Questions can be either open – 'Tell me what you like about your current job' – or closed – 'Do you like your current job?'.

Good interviewers will always ask open questions that encourage you to give a full answer, but it is not a perfect world – not every interviewer is a good interviewer.

brilliant tip

Always give a full answer to a question – never just say 'yes' or 'no'. Respond to every question as if it were an open one, even if the interviewer has slipped up and asked something closed.

Q **Do you like your current job?**

A 'Yes' – this is not very informative.

A 'Yes, I really enjoy most aspects of my current role, especially project development which I took on two years ago.'

In anticipating potential questions and planning brilliant answers, don't forget that some of your answers will automatically lead to a follow-up question from the interviewer. Don't be disconcerted by this; it usually means you have said something that captures their interest and they want to know more. If it is just that they want something clarified, they will say so. The key to success is to rehearse what you want to say, but not learn it off by heart. Recall all your relevant experience, your unique selling points, your personal qualities and strengths and any problem areas you might encounter. Become so familiar with this material that, if someone stopped you in the street and asked you to tell them everything about yourself in the next 60 seconds, you could do so with ease.

Dress for success

Intellectual and psychological preparation for an interview is crucial, but there are other more basic but essential aspects to consider. If you think that some of what follows sounds obvious – it is, but there are still countless candidates who let themselves down by turning up late for interviews, failing to read instructions about what they should bring with them, and appearing in a suit that has not been to the dry cleaners for a year and still bears the evidence of three wedding receptions it has attended.

Good personal presentation is an absolute must. It also makes you feel much better, much more confident and much more in control.

Being dressed for success is essential. It is quite understandable that candidates are anxious. Being too casual might imply that you couldn't care less – being too formal could suggest that you are stuffy and boring.

It is safest to opt for smart and formal. If you turn up for the interview and find that it looks like 'dress down Friday' even though it is a Tuesday, you can dress down when you have secured the post. Your formal dress is unlikely to count against you, whereas being too casual might give the impression that you couldn't really be bothered, and that you are not taking the interview seriously.

brilliant tip

American-run companies and other large multinationals are especially hot on very formal dress, so if you are applying to one of these, be especially particular about your appearance.

Dress may be down to common sense, but it is worth reminding yourself of a few basics. This is especially so if this is the first time you have had to go for job interviews.

You probably don't need these reminders but, for men, wear a suit, a clean shirt and a tie (without a picture of your football team or a photo of your auntie on it). Cleaning shoes appears to be a disappearing art: why not revive it for this occasion?

For women, do wear a suit: a skirt, blouse and jacket or a dress and jacket or a trouser suit. Avoid wearing really high heels.

Everyone should carry a briefcase, smart bag or organiser. Walking in with a plastic bag from a supermarket or a half-finished cup of coffee won't go down particularly well.

Of course, you do need to balance all this advice with what you know about the organisation you are applying to join. A law firm may have a different dress code from a software design company or a food manufacturer but, as has already been stated, when in doubt, opt for formality. Company brochures or websites with photographs of the office or organisation and the staff that work there can give valuable pointers.

It hardly needs to be stated that excellent personal hygiene and good grooming are a must, but even these can catch unwary candidates out. If you have spent the previous evening chomping on garlic bread, quaffing large quantities of alcohol or chain-smoking, you don't want your interviewer to be able to sniff this out.

Even well-prepared candidates can let their standards slip. One human resource director of a large engineering company commented on how many applicants for a whole range of jobs, many at quite senior levels, would appear very well turned out and presentable, with well-polished shoes, smart suit, etc., but with surprisingly dirty finger nails.

brilliant tip

You will make a much better impression if you tell interviewers about your leisure activities, rather than letting them work this out for themselves. If you like gardening or car maintenance, don't let the interviewer discover this through working it out from the clues you are displaying on your hands or your shoes.

If you are using fragrances, opt for small amounts and something very understated. No interviewer likes a cloud of scent to arrive in the interview room two minutes ahead of the candidate. Many human resource professionals advise not using fragrance at all, especially bearing in mind that these can trigger allergic reactions in some interviewers. Avoid heavy make-up, excessive jewellery and boldly displayed body adornments. As always, common sense dictates what will be appropriate; a firm of management consultants will have different expectations to a youth-support project or the cosmetic counter of a leading department store.

Ensure that your wardrobe is organised in plenty of time, that your suit has been dry cleaned, you have respectable shoes and that you are not using a supermarket carrier bag as a rather understated briefcase. Whatever the rules and niceties of dress codes, it is most important that you feel comfortable and at ease.

brilliant tip

However you dress, try to wear something that makes you feel stylish and confident, but you should still feel like you.

Perfect timing

Plan your journey as if you are a pedantic pessimist. Expect the worst that public transport, road congestion, your sat nav and parking restrictions can throw at you. If things do go wrong, as they sometimes will, have the telephone number and contact name for the interview programmed into your mobile, so that you can let them know exactly what is happening. They may well be able to rearrange the time, and the fact that you let them know takes the irritation and frustration out of the situation for them.

Arrive in good time but not too early. Too early is anything that makes you or them feel uncomfortable. Once you know you are in the vicinity, have a cup of tea or coffee, take a stroll, browse round a shop and practise your deep breathing. Once you have arrived at the offices where your interview is to take place, use the few spare minutes constructively, but not frantically. Make a little bit of an assessment of the place.

Here are a few questions to consider to help you assess the organisation you think you want to work for.

- Do the members of staff you meet seem friendly?
- How busy do people appear to be?

- Does the working environment look tidy or chaotic?
- Do people seem stressed and rushed?
- Do people seem relaxed and calm?
- What words would you use to describe the general atmosphere?

Have a look around for any literature about the organisation, its products and services lying around for the browsing visitor. What information can you glean that you have not found out before?

Banish pre-interview nerves

It is a very unusual person who does not suffer from pre-interview nerves, and a limited amount of adrenalin in the system can enhance performance. Interviewers are used to dealing with nerves, but they don't all possess the skill to discern the difference between a slight attack of interview nerves and a nervous temperament. Above all, you want to avoid nerves reaching the stage where they interfere with your performance. How each of us deals with pre-interview tension is to some extent an individual matter, but deep breathing does help and knowing that you have prepared thoroughly and carefully makes a real difference. It may be useful to get a friend or trusted colleague (provided they are not applying for the same position) to ask you some of the questions to which you have prepared answers, so that you can become more at ease with your subject matter.

Say it without words

A good, well-constructed answer to any question loses its impact if that answer is given in a diffident, lacklustre way that doesn't match up to what is being said. The non-verbal clues that you give during an interview say a great deal. This starts from the minute you enter the interview room (or even the building)

– staff you meet there may be giving informal feedback to the interviewer or interview panel. Be pleasant to everyone you meet. Clichés are sometimes truths and a smile really does cost nothing, even if your stomach is churning and your palms feel sticky. It is always a good idea to rinse your hands just before an interview, so that you don't have a clammy handshake. If your file or briefcase is in your left hand, you are ready to shake hands without suddenly having to shuffle everything around. Make sure you use a good, firm handshake without trying to convince the interviewer that you were the national arm-wrestling champion for the past three years.

Nightmare to avoid

One candidate was greatly surprised when a lady dressed in a flowery skirt and cardigan who was offering tea to candidates turned out to be the chair of the interview panel later in the day. How glad the candidate was that she had accepted her tea graciously and had not made a pig of herself with the biscuits.

Seating arrangements in interview rooms vary – in part depending on whether you are being interviewed by one person or by a panel and also according to what your interviewer(s) prefer. Don't take a seat until you are invited to do so, then remember to thank your interviewer. You may find yourself in an easy chair with perhaps a coffee table between you and your interviewer, or you may find yourself on one side of a formal table facing the interview panel across an expanse of desk top and note pads. Don't be daunted – the questions will not be any more or less difficult because of the seating arrangements. When interviewers are taking extensive notes, a more formal set-up is easier for them.

It is difficult if you are sitting in an easy chair, but it is best to sit forward because this makes you look interested and not too casual. Look at the interviewer when you answer questions and if you are being interviewed by a panel look mainly at the person who has asked the question, occasionally glancing in the direction of the others to ensure they feel included in the conversation. If interview panels feel daunting, then bear in mind that you will only be asked the same range of questions as you would be by one person and that they are likely to have arranged in advance who will ask you which questions.

If you know that you have habits such as twiddling your watch strap or earrings, remind yourself to cut these out. Similarly, if you tend to make extravagant hand movements while talking, try to cut these back a little, but you don't need to sit on your hands in a desperate bid to eliminate all evidence of your usual communication style.

Listen carefully before you say anything at all

Most of the advice in this book asks you to think about the answers that you should give to interview questions and to anticipate, as best you can, all the likely questions in the various forms in which they arise. Before you can answer any question, you must make sure that you have really listened to what is being asked. Here's how to be an effective listener:

● Concentrate – don't let nerves stop you hearing what is being said.
● Listen carefully to what you are being asked – rather like reading an exam question before you put pen to paper.
● Don't interrupt your questioner.
● Show that you are listening actively, but ask appropriate questions to help the conversation along.
● Understand your interviewer's point of view, preferably without suggesting that they would benefit from counselling or therapy.

Nightmare to avoid

A candidate who was asked if she had any weaknesses was not
sure if she had heard correctly, but thought she had been asked
if she had any witnesses. This resulted in a confused conversation
where it sounded to the interviewer as if she was summoning
everyone she had ever known to state that of course she was of
good character – the inference being that no, she did not have any
weaknesses. It was only in a rare interview feedback discussion that
this muddle was unpicked.

Don't be discouraged by feeling you have even more to do than
you anticipated: most of these listening skills are those you use
every day in conversations of many kinds – all you need to do is
be aware of them.

Research suggests that the result of many interviews is decided
by interviewers in the first two or three minutes of an interview
and that these decisions are made at an intuitive level and depend
on the rapport that builds up between selector and candidate. If
this is true, then it means that those early aspects of non-verbal
communication – smile, handshake and general demeanor – are
important. There is no mystery to this and the same rules of
courtesy and common sense apply as with any other aspect of
life. What is different is that you probably think about it a great
deal more than you would on other occasions. It is dangerous to
become paranoid about these aspects of your interview, to worry
about whether you have just blown your chances because your
handshake wasn't quite right or that you sat down in your chair
a nanosecond too soon. So long as you remain friendly, warm
and enthusiastic you can't go far wrong.

Summary and reminders

Good preparation is really worthwhile: it allows you to perform more effectively and feel more confident.

1 Double-check your interview date, place and time.

2 Read through your application form and/or CV, or the notes you made during a telephone call.

3 Ensure that you have read any instructions about your interview. Sometimes you are asked to bring something with you or arrive early for a tour of the department or production site.

4 Review your travel plans.

5 Make sure your interview wardrobe is in good order.

6 Complete any research you need to do about the job/organisation.

7 Remind yourself of your key selling points.

8 Switch off your mobile phone — no interviewer wants to know which of your friends is on a train at the moment, or even that you are just about to clinch a big sales deal; there is a time and a place for everything.

9 Be positive – be brilliant.

CHAPTER 2

Make your learning their education

How to show employers what your education really taught you

Your education, to whatever level you have taken it – GCSEs, A-levels, HND, degree, vocational qualifications such as NVQs or professional qualifications – is always something that employers are interested in and will ask about. Their level of interest is determined by how recent and how relevant your education is to the position for which you are applying. If you are fairly new to employment, just out of school or college, questions about your education are likely to form a significant part of the interview. Potential employers will want to know something about your education – something more than the factual information you have provided on your CV or application form. Why did you choose the subject/course/university or college that you attended? What were you good at and what did you find more difficult? Above all, what did you gain from your studies that will be useful to your employer?

brilliant tip

Be aware that not all recruiters are au fait with the many different titles of qualifications. Lists of initials may not mean much – what your course covered and what you did will.

Here are examples of questions and some model answers to consider and adapt to your own situation. Many of these questions are equally relevant if you have just completed a professional training or practical/technical course of some kind.

Again, the interviewer's emphasis is likely to be on how you made your choice, how committed you are to it and whether it is something of specific use to their organisation.

---

brilliant example

Get started by considering this sample question and model answer. The question and answer are followed by a quick analysis of what makes that answer a success.

(Q) If someone who had just finished school asked you whether they should go into employment or carry on with education, how would you advise them?

(A) I would really like to find out more about their own ideas before giving advice, but if I were put on the spot I think I would advise them to carry on with education. Despite the difficulties of financing my studies and the competitive graduate job market, I feel I have learned so much, particularly about taking responsibility for myself and about working with very different groups of people. These are real gains that I believe gave me a good start in my career. People often promise themselves that they will go back and complete their education later on, but I saw how hard this was for some of the students on my course.

Why this answer works:

- You immediately let the interviewer know that you take other people's opinions into account and don't just dole out advice regardless of whether it is wanted.

- The answer acknowledges possible negative issues but gets these out of the way before moving on to the positive.

- The answer includes an upbeat comment about yourself so, although the question was a fairly general one, the interviewee brings it back to the highly personal.

Try analysing some of the answers that follow in this chapter to see why they work. You can use the same technique when you are devising your own model answers.

Ⓠ **How did you choose which university to go to?**

Ⓐ I looked carefully at all those offering the subject I was interested in. I took into account their teaching and examination methods and I also wanted to choose somewhere away from my parents' home where I could learn more about taking responsibility and being independent. I'd also heard some really good things about the facilities and the teaching from school friends who went there a year ahead of me.

Ⓐ I was offered my place through clearing and so my priority was to get a place on a course in psychology/engineering/ business studies. It might not have been my first choice, but it has worked out extremely well for me: it was a good course and gave me a lot of practical knowledge. I could have studied another subject at a university that I would have preferred, but I am glad I stuck to my guns over studying psychology – it is relevant in so many jobs, especially this one.

(It is then likely that your interviewer will follow up with a question such as the following.)

Ⓠ **Tell me why you think your degree in psychology is relevant to the position you have applied for.**

Ⓐ For several reasons; the main one being that I opted for a unit on business psychology where we looked at many aspects of consumer psychology and I am sure that will be useful in your marketing department. Secondly, I had not taken maths beyond my GCSE, and statistics and research methods gave me a chance to develop my numerical skills, and I find I am much better in this area than I had expected. Most of all, I think the course taught me to develop an inquiring attitude to many aspects of human behaviour, something that is applicable in every job.

(For someone who has attended university later on in their career, an answer to this question might be the following.)

Ⓐ I was attending university as a mature student so I had to consider somewhere local. For this reason I looked very carefully at the options on offer and I researched employment records and examination results pretty carefully before I made my choice. I arranged to talk to a course tutor informally before I submitted my formal application.

brilliant tip

Make your answers positive. They fit different life circumstances, but they all show that the candidate took control of their situation, regardless of what limits or constraints they faced.

Ⓠ **Why did you choose to study architecture/ accountancy/law?**

(This question does not only apply to university courses: you can substitute any training course or qualification in a question like this.)

Ⓐ I was very clear that I wanted to study something vocational with a well-defined career path at the end of the course and I was also keen to study something new – something that hadn't formed a large part of my school curriculum.

(In your own situation, you should be able to find something much more personal to say about the specific course you chose: what really triggered off an interest in the subject for you. This something may be related to school or college studies, an interest you have developed or a related piece of work experience you have had.)

ⓠ Why did you choose to study politics/English literature/combined studies?

(In other words, why did you choose something that does not prepare you for a specific career or point you in a specific vocational direction?)

ⓐ I wanted to keep my career options open, study something that I was confident I would enjoy and therefore do well in. I was not ready at that stage to make a career decision, but I was sure that I would acquire a range of useful skills from my studies. I knew I wanted to continue my studies to degree level and I really have enjoyed my course and now I do have a clear sense of direction, which is why I have chosen to apply to you.

ⓠ You are studying biotechnology, but you have applied for a job as a human resources trainee with us – why?

(Do they suspect that opportunities in biotechnology are limited and you have just grabbed at any possible opportunity at random?)

ⓐ I was good at science at school and I thought biotechnology would be an interesting area to work in. I found, though, especially through my various periods of work experience, that I am far more interested in dealing with staff issues and solving business problems than I am in finding scientific solutions. It was a surprise to me, but other people have also commented on my business awareness and how I seem to have a good grasp of personnel issues. My manager in my last work placement mentioned this on my placement report.

ⓠ Would you choose the same course if you had your time again?

ⓐ Yes I would. I enjoyed it, I gained a good degree and I am sure it has helped me develop a range of skills and personal qualities. I write more effectively, organise my time better and know how to seek out relevant information and that is all on top of the academic knowledge I have acquired.

A Well, I might prefer to have done something with a greater emphasis on information technology, but I have really enjoyed my course and I have become very good at working to deadlines, working with others and organising my own workload.

Q **Leaving aside your academic knowledge, what skills have you gained from being at college?**

A I have gained several skills – organising my workload for assignments, researching information, meeting deadlines and working on joint projects with other students have been some of the most significant.

A Returning to university as a mature student, I have learned so much about time management and good planning. I have a young family and I have also taken on part-time work to help my finances. I have met all my deadlines and I expect to do well in my final exams.

A Living away from home for the first time I quickly learned how hard it was to manage on a tight budget, but it has done me a lot of good and I have learned a great deal about taking decisions, solving problems for myself and I think I have gained a lot of common sense.

brilliant tip

Be enthusiastic – all three of these answers are different and highlight a variety of potential benefits. What they have in common is that they are all enthusiastic and all demonstrate that the candidate has thought about what they have gained from their experience. They also emphasise the fact that many jobs and professions are seeking quite similar qualities and skills in their employees.

(Q) We have employed graduates before and they have been fine with ideas, but a bit weak on just getting on with the job. How do I know you wouldn't be like this?

(A) I had a part-time job in a local restaurant while I was studying and that certainly taught me a lot about dealing with customers, fitting in with other staff and spotting where there was work to be done. Working on a joint project with other students, I learned to take responsibility for my particular tasks and discovered how frustrating it is to work with people who don't do their bit. I believe I am offering you a lot of common-sense work skills and my degree is only one part of all that.

(A) I worked in a bank for two years before I went to university, so I was already familiar with a work routine before I started my course. The course has really added to my skills, especially planning my workload, meeting deadlines and working out answers to problems.

(Q) You have been unemployed for quite a while since you completed your degree; how have you remained motivated?

(A) It was easy to be positive at first; after all, many of us are in the same boat. As time went on I realised I had to build some structure into my life and my job hunting. I have also done some work-shadowing which has kept up my enthusiasm. It has not always been easy, but I still feel very optimistic about my chances.

(Q) Which parts of your teacher training course gave you most satisfaction?

(A) The whole course was excellent, but my final teaching practice was really enjoyable. I liked the school where I was based, but my own confidence to deal with pupils and my ideas on how to teach effectively had really developed by this stage of the year, so I was able to put a lot in and get a great deal back.

Q Which parts of your course gave you most satisfaction?

A I was looking forward to the business studies modules on the course, but when it came to it I really enjoyed the practical applications of information technology to solve business problems. My project on developing a specialised database really crystallised this for me.

Nightmare to avoid

One applicant, who was on an environmental management course, decided to bring some lettuces he claimed to have grown as evidence of part of his practical project. His big mistake was to leave these pieces of living evidence of his hard work and success in their supermarket wrappings.

Q Were there any parts of your course that you found difficult?

A To begin with, I found statistics really hard. I had never enjoyed maths very much so it was a real struggle. I am really pleased I had to do this now because my numerical skills have improved greatly and I have learned a lot about how to tackle something I find difficult. I passed statistics with quite a respectable mark in the end.

A At first, being responsible for so much of my own time, it was very different from school and I was not used to it. I attended some study skills classes in my first year and acquired extremely helpful hints and tips on how to plan your work and your time. That sort of thing has become automatic to me now and I enjoy the sense that it is down to me to make something happen and produce the right information in time for a given deadline.

Q **How would you feel about studying part-time while working, if this became necessary in the future?**

A I would be very happy to do this, especially if I were studying something that related directly to what I was doing at work. I like the idea of being able to link practical issues to academic study. I felt that parts of the course I have just completed made much more sense once I had some work experience. I think I would prefer studying something that led to a formal qualification, but this would not be essential.

Q **We were hoping for someone with a degree. Can you convince us that, although you don't have one, you are the right person for the job?**

A I am very confident I could do the job. I did look carefully at the skills you mention in your advert and job description and they seem to match up very well with my experience. My time in administration at the hospital has given me very good organisational skills and a lot of experience in dealing with the public. I worked with some graduate management trainees there and we got on very well. Having a degree, or not, did not seem to be a barrier to working together constructively. Of course, I would be happy to do an evening course in any aspect of management if you felt that this would be useful.

(It is always awkward when adverts say things like 'degree preferred' rather than 'degree essential', because part of you wants to ask why they called you for an interview if they were then going to say that they would prefer someone else. All you can do is keep your cool and be as positive as possible.)

Q **What made you decide that university was the right choice for you?**

A I did think about whether I should work for a year or two first, but I was still enjoying my education. I knew the course I wanted to do and I felt that so long as I did some part-time work to help my finances and give me experience of doing a job, it would be a good decision. I like the idea of being able to get on to the career ladder quickly and really get going.

A I had been impatient to get out of school and start earning money and making a career. I did not mind my job in office admin, but I noticed that new staff who came in with degrees and other qualifications would often start with a more interesting job than mine and I began to think a degree would be useful. Having had a break from studying, I felt a lot more motivated to go back and really get something out of it.

A It was a big decision for me, at the age of 36, but I had always wanted to study law and I had always put earning a living, bringing up my family or other things before my education. It was a shock at first, writing essays, giving seminar presentations and sitting exams, but I have enjoyed it, done well and I know my experience of life and of other jobs has enabled me to develop a lot of common sense and a real ability to work with other people.

Q **I see you went on to do a master's degree immediately after your first degree. Wouldn't some work experience have been more useful?**

A I did weigh up both options, but in the end I decided to complete the academic part of my education and have that extra qualification to offer to employers. I like the idea that I can now concentrate on my job 100 per cent. I have done several part-time jobs in a whole variety of places and these have certainly given me a good grounding in the basics of work. Also, my particular master's course put a strong emphasis on solving practical business problems.

Spend some time working out answers based on some of the ideas outlined above, but which apply directly to your situation. Remember not to sound defensive in explaining your actions and choices. The interviewer is trying to find out how you set about taking decisions, analysing information and assessing your own performance.

Q What was the most difficult assignment you had to tackle while at university/college?

A The most challenging was a 15,000-word dissertation, and the information sources I was using were very varied – the university library, government departments and local businesses. I had to be quite persuasive to get some of the information I needed because I had my deadline to work to and yet I did not want to get on the wrong side of people who were doing me a favour. It was a really useful experience and I am far more confident about planning major projects now.

Q How would you describe the contribution you made to discussions during seminars and tutorials?

A Well, the contribution I made changed and developed during the three years I was there. I was never the person who said the most, but I tried to make sure that what I said was relevant and interesting and I got much better at listening to what other people said as well, rather than just waiting to say my bit. I enjoy exchanging ideas and I can be very successful at persuading someone round to my point of view if I believe it is worthwhile.

(Add an example of an occasion where you have swayed the opinion of a person or a group.)

Q You have said a lot about your course and what you gained from it. What else did you learn from your time at university?

A I was elected as a course representative on our faculty board during my second year. This meant taking responsibility for raising matters of concern to students with senior faculty staff, discussing those issues and, where there was a problem, working with academic staff to produce a solution satisfactory to everyone. One major success I had was in helping to get the library opening hours extended, so that students with family or work commitments could benefit from a more flexible service.

Q How do you prepare to sit examinations?

A By the time I did my final exams I had developed a very clear working method with revision timetables where I would work on preparing briefer and briefer notes on the subjects I was revising and read through these so that they would act as very quick reminders for all the material I was committing to memory. I actually think that some of my assignments were a better preparation for work, because there was still a deadline to be met and information to be researched and presented, which were more of a test of my time management and planning skills than the unseen exams.

Q You seem to have left your job search until after completing your studies. Was this a deliberate choice?

A Yes it was and I know it may seem a slightly risky decision. I really wanted to concentrate on getting the best possible results in my exams. It seems to me that how well you do is very clearly reflected in possible openings in the job market and I did not want to limit my opportunities. It has meant that I have been able to concentrate really hard on the jobs and companies that really interest me, doing plenty of research and even talking to people in the company wherever this is possible. Of course, I was also doing my part-time job and as I had a promotion there during the past six months this has also strengthened my CV and increased my experience.

Q How did you finance your law course/town planning diploma/marketing certificate?

A I had managed to save some money by working for a year immediately after I finished my degree, but I did have to take out a bank loan as well. It would have been great not to have to go into debt, but I got the qualification I wanted and the course was really enjoyable and very practical and relevant, so it was worth borrowing the money.

(Q) **Why did you choose to study on a part-time rather than full-time course?**

(A) It was a difficult choice, because part of me wanted to get on and complete my studies, but I really felt that I would be better off both financially and in career development terms by continuing to work throughout my course and I have worked for the same company for the last two and a half years now. I know I missed out on some aspects of student life, but I compensated for this by making sure I never missed lectures, attending faculty social events whenever I could and developing friendships with students taking the full-time as well as the part-time route on the course.

(Q) **You say you've completed a foundation degree. What's the difference between that and any other degree?**

(A) Well I did mine in two years – it is roughly equivalent to two-thirds of a degree, but it really gave me the chance to work with employers and gain some practical experience working with large IT departments. It was quite intense, so I got used to being extremely busy.

brilliant tip

Never try to sound too clever or make your interviewer feel excluded – it creates a terrible impression. Avoid jargon and don't use confusing acronyms when you are talking about your education. Not all recruiters are familiar with HNDs (higher national diplomas), NVQs (national vocational qualifications), etc. Ensure you and your interviewer both know what you are talking about.

The questions in this chapter give you some idea of the range of subjects likely to be covered. You will also find that many of the questions related to your employment history, your personality, motivation and ambitions will draw on qualities and experience developed through your education – these topics are covered in Chapters 5 and 6.

There are some questions which almost always arise. Work out the ones which apply to your situation and prepare lively, convincing answers.

- Why did I leave school/college at the time I did?
- Why did I choose a particular university/college/training establishment?
- How did I deal with any obstacles that affected my choice?
- Why did I choose my academic subject/training course?
- How does my career choice link to my studies/training?
- If it does not, what explanation do I offer for this?
- What personal qualities has university/college helped me develop?
- What skills has university/college helped me develop?
- What did I enjoy most about my course?
- What was I particularly good at?
- Was there anything I found difficult about my course?
- How did I tackle this difficulty?
- Why did I choose to study, rather than go into employment?
- In what ways has my course prepared me for employment?

Write down answers to any of these questions that are relevant to your situation, so that you become familiar with all the answers and can recall this information without it sounding stilted or rehearsed.

After school

If you have just left school with GCSEs, A levels or NVQs, the questions you face may not be quite so searching, but employers will still be keen to know more about what you studied, what you were good at, what you found difficult or easy and why you took the decisions you did.

Ⓠ Why did you leave school as soon as you had finished your GCSE exams? Why didn't you stay on at school?

(This question won't apply for much longer, since all students will have to remain in some form of education until the age of 18).

Ⓐ I did consider staying on, especially as my GCSE results were quite good, but I had really enjoyed my work experience at one of your hairdressing salons, so I decided I would do well to start on work I enjoyed as soon as possible. I like the idea of learning through work and I know this is a job I want to do.

Ⓠ What differences did you find between being at school and being at college?

Ⓐ I really enjoyed the atmosphere at college, I felt that I was given far more responsibility to get on with my work and, although it was a bit hard at first, I think it really improved my attitude to work.

Ⓠ What made you choose an NVQ in catering rather than opting for A levels? (This is just one example, you could substitute any vocational course for 'catering'.)

Ⓐ I was keen to stay on at school, but I much preferred the idea of doing something that trained me for a particular career rather than something open-ended like A levels. I had a Saturday job in a café and I enjoyed dealing with customers and with food, but I thought this GNVQ would help me to qualify as a really good chef in the longer term.

Q I see you did an A level in general studies; what exactly is this?

A I really enjoyed it. We discussed and wrote about all sorts of current affairs from politics to health care, drug abuse and assisted suicide. It really helped me to put an argument together, but also to listen to other points of view. It has left me determined to vote when I get the opportunity and to become more involved in my local community.

Q Which subjects did you like best?

A English, history and information technology. Information technology is the one I think will be most useful at work. I have had my own PC for five years now and I shall enjoy any job where I get a chance to use IT to a more advanced level and develop my skills further. I would be quite happy to go to evening classes or do short courses to get better qualified.

Q Which subjects were you good at?

A I got my best results in science and maths. We had really good teachers for those subjects, but I don't think they are the subjects I am most interested in using at work, although I know the maths will always be useful. I did fairly well in most subjects though, rather than having one that was much better than the rest.

Q Were there any subjects you weren't very good at?

A Languages. I took French and German, but I found them tricky. I wanted to do well in maths, English and science and that has paid off well as I have passed all three with good grades.

Q If you could take on a subject you have never studied before, what would it be?

A I would take on a new foreign language – Mandarin maybe or perhaps Spanish. I am really keen to work for a company with a strong international base, and I am sure one of these languages would be an asset. I got good grades in French and German, so I think I have a bit of a flair for languages.

Q **What would your teachers say if I asked what your behaviour was like in the classroom?**

A I really think they would say pretty good, especially in the last two years. Once I was working for my exams I really started paying attention and I hardly ever missed school. I think I've grown up a lot in the last year or two.

Q **You've got good A-level results. Why have you decided to apply to us now rather than go to university and apply for our graduate training scheme?**

A I did think about university, but I know I want to join the police force and I really want to learn on the job. I know I would be a bit older if I joined after university, but your training looks very thorough and I want to learn about real situations as quickly as possible.

Regardless of the level to which you took your education, employers will look at how it has contributed to your choice of career and your career progression as well as what skills it has given you that you can use effectively in the workplace. Questions around these two themes will underpin much of what you are asked about your education when you are being interviewed.

brilliant tip

Don't be daunted: remember that none of these questions means the interviewer thinks you have made a bad or wrong decision, they simply want to check that you have looked at the options and

▶

> weighed up the pros and cons carefully. They are looking at your
> attitude to taking responsible decisions that affect your life. They
> need reassurance that you are not going to change your mind a
> few weeks after you have started the job.

This brief questionnaire will help you remind yourself of the skills, qualities and attributes that your education has helped you develop. Score items from 1 to 5.

Slight extent	1	2	3	4	5	Great extent
Personal development						**Score**

1 Ability to learn from your own experience

2 Ability to reflect on your experiences

3 Ability to take decisions

4 Ability to research information

5 Ability to form concepts

6 Ability to learn something new

7 Ability to assess your own strengths and weaknesses

8 Ability to meet deadlines

9 Ability to organise information

10 Ability to plan for the future

11 Ability to come up with imaginative solutions to problems

12 Ability to work cooperatively with other people to achieve a common goal

Familiarity with your education should become second nature to you before you begin discussing it at job interviews.

Summary and reminders

Review your education and be ready to promote your successes and be positive about your choices.

1   If you have examination results, make sure you know what they are.

2   Make sure you can find your certificates. These are not often requested, but it is annoying if they are and you can't find them.

3   If you are awaiting results, give a reasonably accurate, but optimistic, prediction of what you expect to achieve.

4   Talk to the teacher, tutor, lecturer or trainer who you would like to use as your academic or educational referee. If you let them know in advance, they are more likely to say nice things about you and be able to put more thought into what they say.

5   Use the questionnaire in this chapter to organise your responses.

CHAPTER 3

Work to impress

Making your employment history work for you

Your employment history may consist of anything from a Saturday job or a paper round while you were at school to 20-plus years' experience in practical, professional, technical or managerial work in your chosen field. Wherever you are upon this pathway, your employment history is clearly of great interest to your prospective employer. They will want to know how it fits in with your overall career and ambitions, what you have done that may be of direct relevance to the post you are now seeking and what you have learned about your work styles through your previous jobs. They will be looking for evidence of a continual path of development, even though this may include some changes of direction and some sideways rather than upwards moves.

brilliant tip

Employers will want to know what difference you can make if they offer you a job so you must convince them of:

- how well you will get on with your colleagues;
- your ability to see tough assignments and projects through;
- what range of ideas you can contribute;
- how well you motivate others and what kind of team member you are, and
- much, much more.

Which qualities and characteristics they are most interested in will vary according to the type of work you are seeking. The level of expectations they will have is to some extent dictated by how much experience you have had. Whatever the situation, they will expect you to be able to give clear and cogent answers about all aspects of your work experience. Chapter 9 will deal specifically with some of the possible problem areas in your career history, such as losing a job or having a patchy work record. This chapter will focus on common questions likely to be faced by most candidates.

The questions and answers in this chapter draw on examples of candidates who have had very little work experience and those who already have a substantial career behind them. Consider the questions and answers which best reflect your circumstances.

---

brilliant example

Get started by considering this sample question and model answer. The question and answer are followed by a model answer and a quick analysis of what makes that answer a success.

Q How do you measure your success at work?

A My main measure of success is feedback from clients. If they place more orders with us or refer us on to other potential customers, then I feel this is a really useful measure. Keeping clients happy and returning often with more business is probably even more important than getting new clients, at least as a measure of performance. I also use attendance records of staff in my department as a measure of my management success. I would be very worried if my department started to develop high absentee or sickness problems. Having a happy and motivated team instinctively feels like an important indicator for me.

Why this answer works:

● It shows you have good business sense.

- It shows you don't just rely on one measure while ignoring other possible signs.

- You use the opportunity to flag up a couple of good points about yourself – you take your management role and your work with clients very seriously.

- It acknowledges that you need to monitor success for yourself regardless of what other appraisal and monitoring systems are in place.

- It concludes on a nice optimistic note.

Try analysing some of the answers that follow in this chapter to see why they work. You can use the same technique when you are devising your own model answers.

Q I see that you had a Saturday job at your local chemist while you were studying for your GCSEs. What did you learn from this job?

A I found it quite exciting because it was the first job I had ever had. I really enjoyed talking to customers and I had a really helpful manager who took time to explain things about stock control and ordering and all that side of things. I ended up helping with the training when we took on new Saturday staff and I got some extra days there during my school holidays.

Q I notice you took on a part-time job doing data entry while you were a student. How useful was this?

A It was the final year of my course, so I did not want to take on something that was too intellectually challenging and I did need the money. Actually it taught me a great deal about being thorough and being able to cope with repetition when you have to. I was made supervisor for some shifts and I got on really well with other staff and saw how important it is for a team under pressure to work well together. My knowledge of IT meant I could do a little bit of troubleshooting for them too and that was really satisfying.

Ⓠ Did you do any work experience while you were at school?

Ⓐ Yes, I did two weeks at a local transport company booking coach tours; I spent a lot of time on the telephone and learned how to give quotes. It was great; it made a change from school, but it also made me realise it really was worth working for my exams.

brilliant tip

Interviewers should not ask questions that lead you only to say 'yes' or 'no'; if they do, you have to be the one to make up for it.

Ⓠ I see that your business studies course included one year's work experience. What are the three most significant things you learned from that year?

Ⓐ I was delighted to get a placement in the customer relations department of such a large telecommunications company and it really taught me so many things, but the most significant three were how to work as part of a team, to ask the right questions so that I could become effective quickly and, above all, common sense. You can never predict exactly what form an enquiry will take and you don't always have a standard reply, so you have to think on your feet and come up with something sensible.

Ⓠ You have applied for a permanent position with us, but I see that you have been doing temporary jobs for several different companies over the past three years. Why is that?

(The interviewer wants to know whether you have got what it takes to hold down a permanent job.)

A Since deciding to go into hotel management I have always liked the idea of working for an independent operator rather than one of the big chains, so I decided to get as much valuable experience as I could in all aspects of hotel work, while I waited for the right opportunity to come along. As you can see, many of my temporary jobs have been with the big chains and I have learned a lot, but it has confirmed that I do want to work somewhere where there is more scope for individual flair and some very traditional values of old-fashioned customer service too.

A My main reason for temping was that I had not made a really definite decision. I thought I could gain experience of different work environments and the different types of administrative work within various organisations. The experience was really useful and has shown me that I much prefer to work for a smaller company like yours, where I feel far more involved and understand several aspects of your work and your customers. I like being part of a busy team and it brings out the best in me.

Q We can only offer you some short-term contract work at the moment; are you still interested?

A Yes, very much so, especially as I have been really impressed with what I have learned about you this morning. I would hope that you are soon able to offer me something more, but I am quite happy to take that kind of risk. I was very lucky the last time I took on a 'short' contract.

Q Since completing your course at university, you seem to have done mainly bar work and other routine catering jobs. How do you think these are going to help you as a trainee in our IT department?

A The main reason I took those jobs was because I have been studying part-time for a master's course in business information technology and I really wanted to do well in this, as my first degree in American studies isn't so vocational. I have had lots of contact with employers carrying out information interviews for my course project, which has got me in touch with your business. Actually, the catering and bar jobs were useful: you learn so much about customers, about solving problems and about thinking on your feet.

Q **Your CV shows that you have done a lot of voluntary work, but not much paid employment. Why is that?**

(This question leaves you wondering whether they are asking you to outline the benefits of your voluntary experience and relate them to this current application, or suggesting you only work when you feel like it – concentrate on the first option.)

A My voluntary work has been very varied, working in a hospital, for a local community youth group and on an environmental project. At one time I was working on all three at once and ended up with a 50-hour working week. I have learned so much about working in teams, negotiating and being well-organised, but above all it was the fund-raising for these projects that enabled me to clarify that it was in fund-raising, promotional work and marketing that I could see my future career.

brilliant tip

Think in terms of your transferable skills

Transferable skills are exactly what they say – a skill learned in one situation that you can apply in another. If you can solve an engineering problem, you may well be able to apply the same logic to a financial problem. If you can come up with a creative colour scheme to decorate your house, you might have a good design idea for the cover of a leaflet, etc.

Q **I understand you worked without pay for three months for a London law firm; don't you think you are worth a salary?**

A If I had not been confident that I am worth a good salary I would not have worked on such terms. The law is so competitive at the moment and I saw it more as a chance to gain experience, and demonstrate my levels of skill and my enthusiasm. If the firm had not had to start making redundancies, I believe they would have offered me a post on a salary. Things went really well there and they have said they will give me a very good reference.

Q **You have been with your current employer for only 18 months. Why have you decided to make a move now?**

A I took the job because I have an overall interest in product design and it was a really good start for me, even though I had never thought much about lawnmowers before. I had always wanted to get into the motor vehicle industry because rebuilding old cars is a real passion of mine. When I saw that you were advertising I knew it was an opportunity not to be missed. In fact I have learned a lot working with the design team for the past 18 months.

brilliant tip

Spot the common thread that weaves through the answers above – that of transferable skills. If as a candidate you have had what may seem limited or irrelevant work experience, dispense with this notion immediately. No work experience is invalid: it all teaches you something, and getting you to analyse this something is what interviewers do when they ask the kinds of question you have just encountered. Careers counsellors and coaches helping applicants tease out these skills encounter every kind of previous work experience from which to draw out these transferable skills.

Ⓠ **You have been with your current employer for 22 years. What has made you decide to apply elsewhere now?**

Ⓐ That 22 years might have been with one company, but the company has grown, my role within it has changed several times and I have had several promotions while working there. I started off in their accounts department with a manual accounting system and now I am deputy head of purchasing and took responsibility for installing our latest electronic purchasing system. I like the company and I respect the way they work, but I am certainly ready and qualified to take on a job as head of purchasing and I could bring a great deal of experience to your company. I could go on to outline some of my particular skills if you wish.

Ⓐ It sounds a long time when you put it like that and I suppose 22 years in a government department *is* a long time, but my work has been varied and I now manage a department of more than 100 staff. My experience in policy development and as a policy adviser puts me in an ideal position to take on this position with you. My experience in the Civil Service has helped me become very resilient, very thorough and good at interpreting complex information. I am sure I could use these skills very effectively for you.

Ⓠ **You ran your own business for three years. How do you feel you will fit into a situation where you won't have total responsibility for all the decisions, and where work will be delegated to you by somebody else?**

Ⓐ It was exciting running my own catering business and it went well. I built up a substantial base of satisfied customers but it became more and more difficult to compete with new legislation and I think, even more significantly, I actually missed working with other people. I worked for catering companies before I ran my business and when I left I was still enjoying it – I like working in teams and as this is a management job I shall have considerable responsibility, I am sure.

Q I notice you ran a business that had to fold up after two years; what do you think was behind the failure?

A It was the recession – that may sound predictable, but we simply ran into problems with too many other small businesses owing us money. I still gained a lot from the experience; it has taught me to think on my feet and to be resilient under pressure. It has also made me somewhat harder about chasing up money owed, which I am sure you would appreciate in the role I have applied for here.

brilliant tip

To ensure you make a great impression, expect questions that focus on your performance at work, your successes, failures, satisfactions, difficulties and attitudes to clients or customers and relationships with colleagues.

Q What would your current manager say about your work?

A She would say I was a very committed and enthusiastic member of the department. I believe she would mention in particular that I keep calm when there is a lot of pressure and that I don't let attention to detail slip when we are close to a deadline.

brilliant tip

If you sound too wonderful, they may come back at you, so be ready to justify your answer or give further information to back up what you have said.

Q **That all sounds very promising, but if she was then asked to come up with any faults or weaknesses, what might she say?**

A She might say that I sometimes get involved in too many projects at once – that I can get a little bit carried away with enthusiasm and I have to discipline myself to curb that and be even more willing to delegate some projects to others. I have become much more effective at delegation during the past 18 months.

Q **You have been in management for five years now. What might staff who are managed by you say if they were asked to appraise you?**

A I have a great relationship with my staff and I am sure they would pick out the fact that I always try to listen to people's ideas and suggestions regardless of their position within the department. They would say I encourage them to take individual responsibility, but that I am approachable (usually) if they are running into any problems.

(Your answer might provoke a follow-up question – or even the need to reach for a sick bag.)

Q **Would they all be that positive? There must be aspects of your management style that some of them would be less enthusiastic about.**

A I'm not sure that it's my style they sometimes find difficult. I have had to implement some unpopular decisions, for example, introducing evening work rosters that were completely new to our department, and that upset a lot of staff and caused genuine problems for many of them. I think that offering people a full and truthful explanation about why the decision had been made and trying to offer some flexibility in implementing it helped staff to accept the situation, but there are some who are still annoyed about it.

Q You say your staff like you and you all get on well as a team. Does this mean you are a bit of a pushover?

(Be prepared for nasty questions like this that may be sprung on you.)

A No, there is a world of difference between involving staff in consultation and communicating effectively with them, and allowing people to take liberties. My section has one of the best records in the organisation for low absentee rates and time-keeping, and attitudes to taking on extra work are very healthy.

Q If you have had a recent performance appraisal, what has it highlighted as work goals for the coming year?

A Yes, we do have an annual performance appraisal; my most recent one was done four months ago. The main point that came up was that I was ready to take on greater management responsibility and also more responsibility for training new staff. As a follow-up to the appraisal, I have already attended one course on effective management styles and another on dealing with staff disciplinary issues.

Q Have you ever found yourself in a position where you don't get on with a colleague, and how have you tackled this?

A Yes, in the job before my current one I really didn't hit it off with our head of public relations; we were both on the same level, so neither of us could pull rank to solve the problem. In the end I grasped the nettle and persuaded him that we should have a talk and try to work out an effective strategy for us to work together – we really needed to with me working in marketing. We had a pretty frank discussion and, although I can't say we ended up the best of friends, we did gain more respect for one another's roles and we certainly worked more productively together. I was really glad I had taken the initiative.

Q If we asked a colleague of yours to describe a fault you have, what would they come up with?

A My last manager might say I was sometimes a little too impatient with other staff. I find it very frustrating when people don't do their bit, especially if we are trying to meet a deadline. I have learned that taking a bit of time to explain why things must be done now and also reminding people of their obligations to the team does pay off and I get a better response by working in that way, so I have learned a lot about how to get the best out of people and benefited from feeling far less stressed myself.

brilliant tip

Sometimes your reasons for looking for a new position may be that you have had fractious relationships with difficult colleagues. Never state this as your reason for job changing – working relationships are very important to employers since they all link to the 'will you fit in' question.

Q How do you cope under pressure? This is a very busy department you have applied to join.

A I enjoy a certain amount of pressure – it makes me alert and very motivated. There are limits and I try to avoid pressure becoming too great by planning my workload well ahead, but sometimes the unexpected crops up, however well you plan. In my current job as production editor I can have everything ready for the magazine deadline and a client suddenly decides they want to change an advert or a picture – I have to decide whether it's realistically possible to do this without making the magazine late, and if it isn't I have to keep calm and try to ensure that we don't lose the client. That is always a very pressured situation.

A I have worked in social services for eight years now and every department I have worked for has been busy and I have managed a heavy caseload. It is stressful when you are dealing with several difficult cases at once, but I find the most useful way of coping is to talk to colleagues and managers to gain some support and also to learn to switch off and leave work behind when I leave the office. I used to find that difficult, but I find that going for a swim at the end of the day and also doing an evening class in something completely different to the job – I am doing a course in Italian at present – really helps me to switch off and be more effective again the next morning.

(A) Marking examination papers is always one of the most pressured times of year because I have to do it thoroughly and yet there is an absolute deadline. I cope by developing a really clear routine for my marking and by keeping the rest of my life very simple during those weeks. Of course, that's a kind of planned pressure; there's also the unexpected pressure, such as when staff suddenly go off sick or leave and I have to plan all the extra cover for the department and inevitably put pressure on others. Involving people and remembering to thank them helps to soften the blow.

(Q) **How do you cope if a project you are working on goes wrong?**

(A) First, I assess the steps we need to take to minimise the damage limitation and deal with the immediate problem. Once the crisis is over, I analyse what went wrong and I include colleagues in this discussion, so that we can pinpoint how we might avoid the same thing happening again.

brilliant tip

Don't be in a hurry to reveal a weakness or a mistake – you will feel much better concentrating on your good points.

Nightmare to avoid

A highly qualified overseas development manager was on his way to an interview for a prestigious post. He got to the interview late because he drove his Mercedes into the back of a lorry. He telephoned for assistance and managed not to be quite as late as the chair of the interview panel, who apologised but said he had been stuck behind some twit who had driven his car into the back of a lorry and what a pity such people were allowed on the roads. The interviewee chose not to disclose the story.

Perfection is impossible to attain and interviewers know this, but they do want to ascertain that you are capable, confident and willing to do the job. They want that understandable reassurance that they are not about to employ someone with psychopathic tendencies or take on an accountant who will disappear with the company's funds within three months. Clearly, if this is your intention you won't announce it at your interview, but your prospective employer will try both through interviews and, perhaps, through psychological tests to ensure that you are a reasonable human being.

brilliant tip

Consider carefully which weaknesses you choose to reveal when you are asked about these at interview. 'I don't have any at all' is a reply that lacks conviction and immediately lets slip that either arrogance or dishonesty may be among your less pleasing personal qualities. If, however, you believe you may be harbouring psychopathic tendencies, or you absconded with the tea club funds from your last job, this may be a truth better kept to yourself. Consider weaknesses that can be seen as training needs, as areas that may require some development, but you have already begun to work on successfully, or those weaknesses that can be made to sound like strengths: being impatient/enthusiastic about doing a good job, taking on too many projects/being a really hard worker, etc.

All the questions about your work experience link to the fundamental questions mentioned in Chapter 1: Can you do the job? Will you do the job? Will you fit in?

brilliant tip

Take this opportunity before your next interview to think about which of the following words might describe your working style – these will help you construct some of your own answers.

Discerning	Receptive	Assessing	Observing
Productive	Reflecting	Risk-taking	Careful
Practical	Questioning	Active	Responsible
Cooperative	Analytical	Decisive	Supportive
Creative	Thorough	Measured	Dynamic
Efficient	Independent	Imaginative	Committed

Keep in mind that using any of these words in your answers will have far greater effect when you back up your claims with actual situations, problems or challenges you have dealt with.

Ⓠ **Tell me how your experience to date makes you suitable for this job.**

Ⓐ I started as a junior reporter on the local paper I am working for now and it was an excellent way to learn the basic skills of chasing stories, interviewing, writing and following stories up. Education became quite an issue in our area because of various school closures and mergers and that gave me a chance to get really involved in an issue and build up a network of useful contacts and be well-informed. I know all of this would be relevant to a national daily like yours. I feel ready to make the move; it is something I have always wanted and my current editor has been really encouraging, even though he says he does not want to lose me.

(A) Among the many things I have learned from my time as a store manager, I have learned a great deal about our fashion product range: what sells well and items that you think will be great, but just don't seem to have that vital appeal to customers. I enjoy many aspects of management, especially anything connected with display and merchandising, and I think I would contribute really well to the buying department. I think I have a real feel for what customers want and a realistic approach to cost.

(A) I have been a nurse at this hospital for six years now and, because I also have a degree, I am in an ideal position to take advantage of your management training scheme. I love working with patients, but I suppose one of my greatest satisfactions is training and supporting new staff on the ward and helping them to understand how their contribution is essential to both efficiency and high standards of patient care. I would like the opportunity to take this part of my work further and the management scheme would certainly allow me to do this. I think it pays dividends to have some managers who have come up through the grass roots of nursing.

(Q) **What would you say is your greatest strength?**

(A) I am sure it is dealing with people – my interpersonal skills are very good. I seem to be able to pitch myself at just the right level, whether I am presenting something to the management board or solving a problem with a customer on the telephone. I am good at persuading people around to my point of view without bullying them. I always enjoyed debates and discussions at university and I have become a good negotiator.

(A) I am really good at spotting ways in which a process can be carried out more efficiently to save time and money. I managed to cut back the number of procedures involved in our internal ordering system in my current job and, although colleagues said it wouldn't work at first, it is going really well now.

Q **What is your time management like? How do you plan your working week, for example?**

A At the end of the week I make a list of the most important tasks that lie ahead for the following week and decide which I shall tackle first. I usually organise a brief team meeting first thing on a Monday morning, so that anyone can bring up anything they are concerned about or where they feel there are likely to be real pressure points during the week.

Q **How do you set about prioritising your workload?**

A Perhaps I should give you an example. As the head of a department in a large recruitment consultancy, a great deal of post is addressed to me and, although it is partly sorted by other staff, I still face a full in-tray every morning. I quickly sort everything into three piles. The first is things that need to be followed up straight away, for instance vacancies to be processed or new clients to be followed up. I have a second pile of relatively important items, invitations to conferences, internal memos, etc., and a third heap that may well be destined for the rubbish bin – irrelevant product adverts and endless questionnaires.

Q **What action do you take if you have members of staff working for you who really don't get on with one another, to the point where this is affecting other staff?**

A I make my own assessment of where faults might lie, but I get those staff together in a meeting and give them an opportunity to raise what they find difficult about their colleague, without allowing blatant insults, and then I ask them to suggest things to make the situation work better. Of course, this is assuming they are both good employees and that there are faults on both sides. If it is simply a case of one person behaving unreasonably, then I would outline my dissatisfactions and ask them to make some improvements.

Q **What sort of contribution do you make to a team or work group?**

A Having graduated last year, I am fairly new to work teams, but I took part in two group projects while on my engineering course. On one project I was asked to lead and I found it quite a challenge motivating other team members so that they all pulled their weight. I learned how vital it is for people to really understand their specific tasks and to realise how these relate to the whole project. In my second group project I had specific responsibility for industrial liaison, gathering data from employers and working closely with them. I got a lot out of this, but I preferred the role of team leader.

Q **What is the most difficult situation you have had to deal with at work and how successful were you in dealing with it?**

A When I was working as head of finance in an educational organisation, I had to implement a 3 per cent cut in our annual budget across all departments, and it was my task to work out how this cut should be shared across all departments: whether some should bear greater or smaller reductions, rather than simply implementing a blanket cut. It was hard because I was new; it was an unpopular policy and everyone was trying hard to convince me that they should be spared from the burden of the cuts. I kept a clear head, undertook a thorough analysis of the previous year's cuts and potential income-generating activities in each department and I ensured that my decision was transparent and understood by everyone. I was not popular with all departments, but our finances improved in the following year, which really vindicated my actions.

Q **What is the most satisfying aspect of your current job?**

A I continue to enjoy dealing with patients and their families, but I think over the past two years developing induction and training programmes for new members of staff has given me the greatest satisfaction and enjoyment. It seems to me that if staff get good training and support from the minute they join us, then patient care will be of a higher standard and those staff will, in turn, get much more from their work.

(A) Managing to get a really major client on board to advertise with us has been a real thrill. We had tried several times in the past and they had always eluded us, but I must have put together just the right package and offered them the right price, because they are now a big source of income for us and the relationship with them is going really well.

(Q) **Is there anything you don't like about your current job?**

(A) I have to confess that I don't like some of the routine paper work, especially since, in my opinion, a lot of it could be replaced with an on-screen system. I have developed the attitude of getting it done quickly, so that it doesn't pile up or get behind and that's the way I've tried to make it more palatable, even if I can't say it's exactly exciting.

(Q) **Describe a situation where you have had to deal with an angry customer/client/member of the public. How did you cope and what was the outcome?**

(A) You do get angry customers in restaurants and on one occasion a regular customer who often brought business clients for lunch suddenly went really wild complaining that their wine was off and that they had had to wait for too long for their meal. He was really shouting and everyone stopped eating and looked round. It was the manager's day off so I had to deal with him. I kept very calm, spoke quietly and immediately offered them another bottle of wine. I apologised for the delay and explained that it was because all the meals were freshly prepared and that a soufflé always took a few extra minutes. I think he was just having a bad day because he calmed down pretty quickly.

Ⓐ My last company built some specialist software for a client to handle its database. The client kept altering their requirements and as a result we had not got the system up and running for them by the agreed date. As I was the sales consultant who'd dealt with them to begin with, it fell to me to placate them and it was not easy. I think being prepared to apologise straight away helped and I also arranged a deal where we offered some additional systems support – a little more than had been agreed in the original contract. Of course, I got clearance to do this from my managing director.

Ⓐ A father became really angry and abusive at a parents' evening once because his daughter had not had a very good school report – I was her class teacher at the time. She was a disruptive pupil and had not done very well, although I had tried to give her attention and support. It was very unpleasant, but I tried to get him talking about the things she was better at and why they were working well and what she enjoyed at home and, as soon as we got into a proper conversation where he realised I knew who his daughter was and she wasn't just a number or a box to be ticked, then things calmed down pretty quickly. He became more involved in her schooling after that.

Ⓠ **What would you do if someone uncovered a mistake you had made?**

Ⓐ If I was genuinely unaware that I had made this mistake, then I would apologise straight away and offer to do anything I could to put the matter right or minimise any negative effects that my actions had caused. I mean, if it meant apologising to a client, then I would do this rather than try to pass the buck or pretend it was not my fault. That's how I would want people who work for me to behave and I would set exactly the same standards for myself.

Q What would you do if you realised you had done something with potentially serious consequences for your employer?

A Fortunately, this is not an experience I have had and I hope it never will be. If this did happen, then the first thing I would do would be to go and speak to my line manager and be really up-front about what I had done, or forgotten to do, and be as helpful and open as I could about the situation. I would try not to blame other people, but if I had been let down by colleagues in various ways, then I would have to be open about this too. I would certainly offer to do anything I could to rectify the situation. If there were systems failings that had contributed to the problem, then I might suggest changes. Fundamentally, though, if I were in the wrong, I would own up to it.

Q How would you go about building relationships with new work colleagues?

A I think the key when you join a new group or meet other groups of colleagues is to listen and pay attention to what they say and what their concerns are. It is important to make some contributions, suggestions or comments fairly early on, but I don't express too many opinions until I have done some careful listening and reflected on what I have heard. Taking opportunities to be helpful is also useful: you get to know individuals and you find out about any problems, busy times and possible causes of stress.

Of course, not every awkward encounter in your working history will have had such successful and happy outcomes as these three, but what the interviewer wants to know is how you dealt with the situation, what strategies and tactics you employed to try to bring about a good result, even if, sometimes, it does not work.

Remember, all the questions and answers in this chapter will vary according to the job you are applying for.

brilliant tip

Stress the skills and qualities most appropriate to the job. If you are being interviewed for a position as somebody's personal assistant, then alarm bells will ring if you announce that you feel you are a natural leader and like to take firm control of situations. If you are being interviewed to lead a project or head up a department, then by all means stress your skills of listening, involving other people in the decision process and being aware of other people's strengths, but ultimately you are there to lead, to motivate and to take responsibility for ensuring that the job is done on time or that your department runs smoothly and effectively.

The key to answering many of these questions successfully is in being able to illustrate your answers with accounts of situations taken from your past and current work. If you say you cope well working under pressure, give an example of when you have done this. If you say you are an effective team leader, you should describe a team you have led and how you were effective. Never assume that the interviewer knows any of this – they may be skilled, but they are not telepathic.

A constructive way to plan your answers to these questions is to look at your employment history and list some of the most valuable learning points from each job you have held.

> ### brilliant tip
>
> The following chart will help you organise information about your employment history and become familiar with it. It can double up to help you formulate your CV or complete an application form.
>
> | Employment history | What I learned | What I achieved | What I found difficult |
> | --- | --- | --- | --- |
> | Current job | | | |
> | Previous job 1 | | | |
> | Previous job 2 | | | |
> | Previous job 3 | | | |
>
> Add further jobs if you wish to.

Questions aren't always asked in neat categories relating to education, employment history, etc., but this is a useful way to organise your responses.

Summary and reminders

Use your employment history, however short, however long, to put across all the experience you have gained.

1 Check your CV or application form, paper or electronic, to remind yourself of exactly what your employment history comprises.

2 Don't discount experiences such as voluntary work or brief periods of work experience – this is especially important if you have only a brief job history.

3 If you have helpful colleagues, friends or managers, talk
   to them about your faults and your strengths to clarify
   the picture for yourself. You may discover good points you
   weren't even aware of and, if you discover any bad ones,
   you don't need to share these at an interview.

4 Spend much more time thinking about your strengths and
   successes than your flaws and failures.

5 Ensure that you use a range of situations to demonstrate
   your selling points; don't build all your answers around one
   project or one incident.

CHAPTER 4

Is this the place for you?

What you need to know
and how to let them know
you know

t is reasonable for employers to wish to know why you have approached them with your application. Anyway, you have told them a lot about you, through your application, so why shouldn't you have some valuable information too? In reality, you may be making multiple applications, especially if you are really keen on a change of job or career or if you have just completed your education or professional training. Even so, every employer wants to feel that they have been chosen and specially selected by you. They know that you are probably shopping around, but you still need those convincing arguments and that winning flattery at hand. Careful thought and intelligent research will prepare you to answer all their likely questions on this topic.

brilliant tip

Whatever type of work you are chasing, carry out as much research as you can before you go to the interview. In this way, you are well informed so you can answer those questions designed to find out how much effort you have put in before the interview. What is more, you have a much clearer idea of what you still want to find out at the interview. This is especially important when you are faced with 'Are there any questions you would like to ask us?' Find out more about this in Chapter 11.

This necessity for research applies whether you are approaching a global corporation, a small IT company, a school, a design studio, a newspaper or the shop round the corner. Obviously how much research you can realistically undertake is going to vary.

brilliant tip

Remind yourself of all the resources you can use to find out more about employers:

- Company or organisation's own websites.
- Other websites, blogs, Twitter, Facebook, etc., offering relevant information (be aware of the difference between information and personal opinion).
- Company brochures, product information, etc.
- Company annual reports.
- Local, national, specialist and trade press.
- Reference and specialist libraries.
- Jobcentre Plus offices.
- Recruitment agencies, careers services and job centres.
- University and college careers centres.
- Word of mouth.
- Your own direct experience of an organisation as a customer, visitor or user of some kind.

Before considering the following questions and answers, be very clear about why the interviewer is asking them. They want to know whether you have put any effort into finding out about them, whether you really have considered carefully the kind of organisation they are – their products, their status, their image, etc. They are not seeking evidence about just how much information you can remember – a few intelligent thoughts and comments will go much further than being able to quote large chunks of last year's annual report from memory.

brilliant example

Get started by considering this sample question and model answer. The question and answer are followed by a quick analysis of what makes that answer a success.

Q What do you consider is our most valuable resource?

A I am sure that the people who work for you are your most valuable resource. In my experience, recruiting and holding on to good staff affects everything you do. It is easier to get a new piece of equipment or software package than it is to replace a team member who is really motivated and works well with everyone else. Talking to people today I have been really impressed with how much emphasis you put on staff training and development here.

Why this answer works:

There is rarely a 'right' answer at an interview, but it is widely accepted that human resources are the key to success of almost any kind of enterprise; therefore, you probably would not do well to suggest that having a nice car park or even a good accounting system is the road to success.

- This answer shows that you have thought seriously about what makes organisations tick, or that you have at least read the right kind of reports.
- It shows that you rate people skills as being important and this bodes well as a guide to how you are likely to work with colleagues and how you value good staff.
- It manages to pay your would-be employer a compliment.

Try analysing some of the answers that follow in this chapter to see why they work. You can use the same technique when you are devising your own model answers.

Q What do you think of our company/organisation?

A I have been aware of your existence as a major clearing bank for a long time. I really liked your recent advertising campaign, and being an Internet enthusiast I was impressed that you were one of the first to set up online banking. It was the main reason I chose to change my bank, so I have experience from the other side of the fence – from being one of your customers.

A I had already decided that I wanted to teach in an inner-city school. It helped that you were happy to allow me an informal visit before I put in my application and I thought there was a really happy atmosphere in all the classrooms I visited. I am keen to work in a school which involves parents and the local community, and your recent fund-raising concert demonstrated that very clearly. It was really enjoyable too – I was part of the audience and it's great to see music being given a high priority.

A I have often popped in here for a coffee and a sandwich. The place has always been bright and clean and the staff here seem friendly and efficient. I like the range of food you offer and the fact that you seem to be on really good terms with so many of your customers.

A I began to notice your products advertised frequently in *Software Today* and I started to sit up and take notice. The fact that you seem to put so much energy into designing specialist software for individual clients really interests me. I like the idea of using my technical skills to work closely with customers.

A Your website is really informative and has shown me a great deal about your products and your proposed future developments. I am very excited by the idea of working for a smaller company where my ideas can make a real contribution.

brilliant tip

Notice how, to make the best possible impression, all these answers, though geared to different employers, have two things in common. First, they demonstrate that candidates have thought about who they are applying to within a particular job market and, second, each candidate took the opportunity to throw in a positive comment to highlight either their suitability or their enthusiasm for the organisation or the position on offer. Ask yourself, could you do this at your next interview?

Q Are we your first choice?

A Yes, although I am applying to other similar firms, I had really hoped to do a work placement with you after I met one of your managers at a recruitment event. You seem to give people a lot of responsibility early on and that does appeal.

Nightmare to avoid

'I read your last three annual reports cover to cover and I wonder if you would like me to quote the annual turnover for those three years for both your widgets and thingies departments separately or possibly as an aggregate figure, or perhaps ...' The interviewers will probably be asleep by now and, on the whole, interviewers should not be bored into submission.

Q Tell me what you know about this organisation.

A I did a three-week placement in your accounts department and that gave me a lot of contact with all your internal departments and that was really informative about what projects you have under way. It also meant I found out a lot about who your customers are and, although my real interest is in marketing, it was a really valuable experience.

Ⓐ When I started looking for work with housing associations I arranged informal visits with those who were willing to allow this. Your colleagues were really helpful in arranging a visit for me, not just to your head office but also to two of your projects, one for older people and one for single-parent families. The projects seemed to be working really well and staff at your main office are incredibly committed to what they are doing – I found that encouraging and quite inspiring – very much the kind of team with whom I'd like to work.

Ⓐ I read your entry in *Advertising World Annual Directory* and noticed that, for a comparatively small firm, you deal with an interesting range of clients. I visited your website and found out more about some of your campaigns for small charities and pressure groups. I could say more about what caught my attention about those campaigns if you would like me to.

(These are all quite different answers, but all make it clear to the interviewer that the candidate has made a positive choice about this organisation and has carried out some appropriate research to support their decision.)

brilliant tip

If you find that sometimes, whatever the topic, you are heading for a potentially lengthy or complex answer, it is a good idea to draw breath and check with the interviewer whether they would like you to say more. If they decline your offer, don't feel crestfallen and foolish; you may already have said enough to convince them, or they may have specific questions they wish to ask you later that explore the topic you have been covering. To ask what the interviewer would like also shows you are confident and in control of yourself.

**Q Are you familiar with any of our products/services/
projects?**

A Yes, several, but particularly your microwave meals and
your soft drinks range – I'm a real fan of some of your fla-
voured mineral waters. Since I started taking an interest in
your company, I have taken note of where your products are
placed on supermarket shelves and observed which groups of
customers seem drawn to them. I could say a little more if you
wish.

A I first found out about your local youth theatre projects
during our local arts week last summer when I saw your production of *Blood Wedding*. I was interested in arts and theatre
administration then, so I took the opportunity to talk to some of
the cast and some of the staff backstage. Since then I've followed
up on several of your community projects.

A At present I am not as familiar with your product range as I
would like to be, but I am quick at assimilating knowledge and
information and I would certainly enjoy learning more about all
the products you supply.

(This last answer is not ideal, but it is better then making something up because if you do say something bland like 'Yes, I think
all your products are excellent', then you are likely to be asked
something like 'What do you think is so good about them?' or
'Which one do you like best then?' and you are going to feel
unbelievably foolish if you have to say you don't know.)

Q How would you rate us against our competitors?

A I certainly think you're the best of the three free newspapers
that are delivered around here. You all have to make money
from advertising and yet you manage to include far more interesting editorial and many more stories that really do concern
local issues – I think that makes a real difference.

(A) Well, once I had decided I wanted to get into management in the fast-food industry I looked at several of the major players and considered their products, their premises, their customer groups and their business performance. Compared with the other pizza chains, I think your outlets look really clean and bright, the service is friendly and you do seem to try to preserve a slightly more authentic Italian feel and that really appeals to me.

(Q) **If you had a free hand, how would you like to see us develop over the next three years?**

(A) I know that you are investing heavily in research and development and I would certainly continue to develop that emphasis. I would like to see you develop further into some of the European markets where Germany and Italy seem to have quite a strong grip at the moment – perhaps you should have more European satellite offices.

(A) The growing market for organic and environmentally friendly products is very significant, I believe, and it is not an area that your company has touched on all that much. I would like to investigate the production costs and the feasibility of developing some of these – I am sure that market will grow significantly over the next few years.

(Q) **What do you think is the most exciting aspect of our work?**

(A) I am very interested in your African development. My father worked in Africa for a while when I was in my early teens and I have a real feeling for the place and, of course, it is a really interesting new market too.

(A) I have read several articles in the press about your recent projects in inner cities working with homeless families. The projects looked really innovative and this was a subject I researched and wrote about for my final-year dissertation at university. I'd be really interested to see how those projects work in the longer term and I would love to be involved with that kind of work.

(A) So many City law firms seem to concentrate only on commercial clients, but you have departments dealing with a whole range of different aspects of the law. My particular interest in environmental law makes you an obvious choice for me and you have been involved in some really high-profile cases in that area.

Nightmare to avoid

Don't make assumptions about the kind of organisation you are applying to. One candidate unwisely told the interview panel that he had applied for the job because he was tired and he thought things might be fairly easy going and he could have a bit of a rest. In fact, it was a busy education department that had just undergone staff cuts and had significantly increased workloads.

(Q) **What do you think of our website?**

(A) I think it is excellent; it's easy to locate the information you want and very informative. If it were up to me, I might be inclined to include a few more photographs.

(Q) **How would you change our website?**

(A) I would like to see the customer payments section made more secure – I have had a bad experience myself with a similar system. I like the way your products are listed and displayed and it is easy to navigate.

(Q) **What do you think of our graduate recruitment information and application procedure?**

(A) I like the way you included the series of profiles of recent graduates on your website, outlining their background and their career development within the company. I would like to have seen one or two more profiles from the technical side, which would have been especially helpful for me since I am applying for R&D. Of course the online application was tough, but I felt the range of questions really gave me a chance to outline my experience.

(Q) **What advantages do you think we have in the market place?**

(A) You have a smaller range of products than some of your competitors, but those products have a deserved reputation for being of a high quality, and your advertising and promotion campaigns mean that people are well aware of these products. I am sure it has been cost-effective for you to gear your production in this direction and last year's figures certainly bear that out, especially given the current problems in the market.

(A) Living in the town, I know exactly which other restaurants around here are your main competitors and I must confess to having eaten at all of them at one time or another. It says a great deal that you always have to book here at least two weeks ahead for a Friday and Saturday night and it goes without saying that I think the cuisine is wonderful – really interesting with plenty of use of fresh local produce. That is one of the many reasons I have applied to be your assistant chef.

(Q) **How do you think we can remain successful?**

(A) You have a strong client base and it is important to keep those clients very happy so that they return to you for their business. Good follow-up service is key here. Of course, you want to extend that client base too and effective marketing is important, but then you need to continue to ensure that every aspect of the business backs up those sales and marketing promises. Every employee has their part to play in this, I believe.

Q Is there anything you think we do badly?

A I'd like to turn that round and look at anything that you might do better, since I am sure you wouldn't enjoy your current success if you were doing anything really wrong. I am surprised that I don't see your products mentioned more frequently in some of the trade press. I know you have a strong customer base, but it can never be a bad thing to extend that.

A I certainly wouldn't say 'badly' – I wouldn't be applying to join you if I had too many concerns in that direction. I have been a customer of yours in the past and I have sometimes found staff dealing with telephone calls unable to help me, or unsure who to refer me to, which makes me want to look at some of your staff-training procedures. You provide a good service and it is important to let potential customers have the information they need with the minimum of difficulty.

Q How do you think we could save money?

A I know this is on everyone's minds at the moment. I wonder how much you spend on external PR consultants and whether we could do that in-house in the marketing department? Perhaps you could look at advertising in fewer magazines – I would need to have more details, but think you could make some savings here. From what I know, you have pared your admin side down already, so we would have to look at other areas.

Q What do you think is the main reason why some companies fail?

A I am sure there are many reasons, but one is probably poor communication between people who design products or develop ideas and the organisation's customers. This really means ensuring excellent internal communication – I am sure this is key to solving very many problems.

Genuine and thoughtful criticism is acceptable – after all, your ideas and input may be about to contribute to the company's success. However, saying everything they do and have ever done is wonderful does not show any insight, imagination or confidence; it does not show that you have really thought about their business, their clients or their market place. On the other hand, no interviewer wants to be told that the organisation he or she works for is out of date, disorganised, has poor industrial relations and is generally hopeless. Your answers need to demonstrate that you have thought carefully about the organisation you are applying to join and have undertaken what information gathering you reasonably can, and applied that to come up with some cogent answers. You really want them to think your brain would be an asset to them.

How much research you can be expected to do before an interview depends on the kind of organisation you are seeking to join. A large business is likely to have an extensive website and to produce reports and brochures and information packs. A very small enterprise may not offer much in the way of tangible information, though most do have websites. Interview candidates are often reluctant to approach companies to see what information is available. They imagine it displays some sort of weakness not to have been able to locate such information from some other mysterious resource. The contrary is the case; no-one is going to lose marks for using initiative and a company is often very happy to send information they have or, on some occasions, to allow you to have an informal discussion with someone, on the telephone or through a visit, before you attend your formal interview. There is never any harm in asking. The very worst that can happen is that you can be told 'No'.

By all means add questions of your own, and some of the above questions will not be appropriate if you are applying to some types of organisation. For example, while it is easy to find large quantities of information about the Civil Service or a multi-national company, information may be more limited in the case of a local small business or a project funded by a charity. Nevertheless, it is a useful discipline to see just how much you do know about your prospective employer.

brilliant tip

Review the list of possible information resources at the start of this chapter, to see what may be helpful for you as you prepare for each job interview.

It may be the right place for you, but are you the right person to work there?

Many of the questions in the first half of this chapter focus on what you know about the organisation you are hoping to join. If you are on the ball and, as your interview technique becomes better and better, you will be able to weave some personal selling points into the answers you give to those questions – in exactly the way that the model answers demonstrate. You will, however, also find yourself being asked quite similar sounding questions, but questions where the focus is much more on you and why *you* believe this particular employer is suitable for you.

Ⓠ **Why do you want to work for us?**

Ⓐ I had an open mind at the beginning of my final year at university, apart from knowing that I wanted to join a large company with a good reputation, and I was simply looking at a range of recruitment information and websites. One of the things that stood out about you was the flexibility you have in offering new staff training in several areas before they are definitely committed to one area.

Ⓠ **What is it about this company/organisation that makes you think you will remain interested and enthusiastic over a long period of time?**

Ⓐ Communications technology is changing so rapidly and, as you are a small company working in a highly specialised area of the market, I can foresee that the new developments here are going to happen frequently for some time to come. I am really committed to the idea of working on research and development for a smaller company – I'm sure it provides a really good opportunity to work closely with other departments and get customer feedback more quickly. I like the atmosphere here too; everyone seems really keen and busy, but there is a real feeling that people are enjoying themselves and everyone has been very friendly.

Ⓠ **We have several clubs and a lot of social activities for staff here. How do you feel about socialising with colleagues?**

Ⓐ I think that always says something good about a company – people will only do this if they want to. I am still friends with colleagues from some of my former posts, and I think it is great to get to know people outside the office and see another side to them. I would describe myself as a sociable person anyway, and I am always happy to join in anything like quiz nights, meals out, or whatever. What social clubs do you have at the moment?

Ⓠ **Who else are you applying to?**

Ⓐ All the other leading firms of accountants, but I would far rather work for you if I had the choice. I attended one of your recruitment events and had a chance to talk to staff who you have taken on recently and I am really impressed with the support you give for professional training and qualifications. Even more important to me though, is knowing you have such a large and successful computer auditing department. That is something which really interests me and would really bring my IT skills and my interest in accounting together.

(A) I have really applied to anything that might help me get my foot in the door because anything to do with arts and theatre is so competitive that I don't think I ought to be too choosy – I accept I will have to work my way up. That's not to say I am not a very strong applicant – I have helped out voluntarily with our last two local arts weeks and of course there's the box office job I had last summer at the Wild Side Theatre. I am really interested in this administrative job you are offering – my experience to date suits it very well.

(A) No, I have drawn up a list of other companies that would interest me and I have my CVs all ready to go but, after having had a part-time job with you for a while last year, I felt I would really like to work for you. Although it is taking a bit of a risk, I would rather see how things went with my application to you, before I send off any more CVs.

brilliant tip

The head of recruitment for a large retail chain recently commented that many graduates seemed to have applied for anything and everything and it made it hard to work out how they really felt about her company. If you do have to apply very widely, find a way to describe your strategy so that it appears focused.

(Q) **Have you received job offers from anyone else?**

(A) No, not so far, although I do have another interview to go to on Friday.

(A) Yes, I have just received an offer from Spring Fresh Foods to join their product development division, but I am more interested in your product range and I'm also impressed by your record on environmental issues.

Q **If one of our competitors offered you a job now, would you accept?**

A I would have to look very carefully at exactly what they were offering, not simply in terms of financial reward, but how relevant it was to my experience and how it might develop my career, but I would really much prefer to work here if I were given the opportunity.

An interviewer is not going to base his or her decision on whether to make you a job offer on what other applications you have in the pipeline, but examining your job-hunting strategy is another way of assessing some of your planning, decision-making and analytical skills. If they are impressed with you at interview, it will be of interest to them that other people may be making you offers and that they could lose out. Don't take any unwise gambles on this one though, like saying you have had other offers if you haven't: if you are level-pegging with another candidate (and this can happen, especially where several staff are being taken on at the same time), they may decide you are a lost cause.

Summary and reminders

Try to find out as much as you can about your prospective employer: after all they will want to find out a great deal about you.

1 Do your research in advance whenever possible.
2 If you really can't do this, make use of the time immediately before your interview either by talking to members of staff or taking note of any publicity about the organisation and its customers that you can find.

3 Remember that all this hard work before the interview
   benefits you too – it helps you work out whether they are
   the right employers for you, not just whether they think you
   are suitable for them.

CHAPTER 5

The personal touch

All about what makes you tick and why this matters

I n Chapter 1, which dealt with being thoroughly prepared for interviews, the point was made that what employers really want to know about is you, every aspect of you and, most particularly, what kind of person you are and whether you will fit in to the job for which you are applying. Will you get on with other staff, or do you have tantrums when somebody asks you to do something you would rather not? Do colleagues and customers see you as a prime candidate for an anger management course? Only the most unwise interviewee would, of course, admit to any of these faults during a selection interview, even if the odd lapses have crept into their working life. Interviewers often focus their questions on trying to discover exactly what makes you tick and whether your traits will combine effectively and efficiently with the work, the ethos, the direction and the general style of your would-be employer.

Of course, they will glean much of this knowledge from the questions you answer about your current and past employment, your education and the reasons behind your career decisions and career progression, but they may also use some more direct questions to find out more about you.

---

brilliant example

Get started by considering this sample question and model answer. The question and answer are followed by a quick analysis of what makes that answer a success.

▶

Ⓐ Describe a contribution that you have made to an organisation outside work and say how your contribution has benefited that organisation.

Ⓐ I am on the committee of a local group that writes, produces and distributes a community newsletter. I have special responsibility for generating advertising because the letter is distributed free to 500 local households. When I joined the group, we were really struggling to generate income. This was partly because the advertising charges were just too low. While we can't charge much, I felt that we could increase our rates quite substantially and still keep all our advertisers and possibly get a few more. Some members were worried that we would alienate people, but I was sure our rates were so low that we would probably find making an increase quite easy. I took time to visit several small local businesses and our advertising revenue has doubled in the past 18 months. I am really pleased; having a good source of local information is very valuable.

Why this answer works:
- It is interesting and will probably grab the interviewer's attention.
- It says something about how dynamic you are – you get things done.
- It says you are a problem solver.
- It says you join in local initiatives, so hopefully you will also be positive about work issues.
- It suggests that you commit to things, but it does not suggest that this outside activity is going to intrude on your working life.
- It ends on an upbeat note with a story of success.

Try analysing some of the answers that follow in this chapter to see why they work. You can use the same technique when you are devising your own model answers.

brilliant tip

You can really turn this next and seemingly daunting question to your advantage. First, it is likely to confront you early in the interview so you will not have used up all your good material as answers to other questions. Second, this is a great opportunity for you to take control – you have the chance to elucidate some of the positive points about yourself that you have planned to include in your interview.

These suggested answers are only openings to what will form part of longer answers that reflect your situation. What they do include, which you should also aim for, is a clear starting point, so that the interviewer is aware of what to expect and has the chance to agree that this is OK. It also gives you the opportunity to go on to some other aspects of your life and your personality if you want to. It is perfectly acceptable to give some information and then ask: 'Would you like me to say a little more about that?', or 'I could tell you a little more about my career aspirations', or 'I could tell you something about what provides the satisfaction for me in any job I am doing'. In other words, if there is a great deal that you could say, don't indulge in a 15-minute monologue, only pausing to check that the interviewer hasn't sloped off for a coffee. Give your answer in discrete chunks, checking at each stage whether they want more.

It may be helpful as part of your interview preparation to ask friends or colleagues how they would describe you – sometimes you become so familiar with yourself, especially if you haven't been asked this type of question for some years, that you find it quite strange to be asked to describe yourself in this way, and the opinions of others can be good reminders and, hopefully, confidence boosters too.

Q **Tell me something about yourself.**

A Perhaps I should begin by telling you why I have chosen to apply to you for this job at this stage in my career and outline how my experience in my current and previous jobs relates to this post.

A I'll start by telling you something about the course I have just completed, what I have gained from it and how it links in with my plans for the future.

A Maybe I should start by telling you one or two of the more unusual things that I have done, what I think I have learned from them and how they would be useful to you if I were to be offered a post here.

(These 'unusual' things could be particular work projects, experiences from voluntary activities or even leisure interests, so long as you make your answer relevant and interesting.)

A Well, I could begin by describing the sort of person I think I am, or at least how friends and colleagues would describe me and then I can give you a bit more about my history if that is helpful.

This seemingly simple request to tell an interviewer something about yourself is one of the most forbidding to interviewees and one you would do well to anticipate. The reason it is so difficult is because you are simply unsure of where to begin, what to include, how much to include and how long to go on for. You can reasonably assume that your interviewer is not expecting an unexpurgated version of your autobiography beginning with your earliest memory of when you left your teddy bear in the park and culminating with the dinner party you held last Saturday, but that still does not answer the tricky question of exactly which choice tit-bits to pick out to whet your interviewer's appetite.

Q What would you say is your greatest achievement to date?

A Being asked to manage the department I currently run has been extremely significant for me. I had been working there for only two years and I had assumed that someone with more experience than me would be asked. I had worked hard and put a lot of energy into developing and expanding our customer base. But I had not anticipated a reward coming quite so soon. The real achievement for me is that I have managed to do this and avoid resentment from other staff who might have assumed that they would be asked to do the job.

A I have to say it has been getting my pilot's licence. I know it is not exactly an everyday skill for this office, but it was an ambition I had held for years; it cost me a lot of money, but it was so exciting when I actually started flying solo and was able to take friends for flights.

A Achieving a university degree at the age of 37 while bringing up a family of 3 and holding down a part-time job to help pay the bills. I had not been all that successful academically at school and yet I found I did really well on my course. My results bear that out, and it has been worth all the hard work and opened up my career options significantly.

A To be honest – giving up smoking. I never thought I could do it and I had had dozens of attempts that ended in failure. It isn't just the fact that I don't smoke any more, I have gained so much personal insight and I deal with potentially stressful situations at work so much more effectively now. I feel more energetic, more mentally alert and far calmer than I ever did before. I even managed it before the smoking ban came into force!

brilliant tip

Cast your net widely – think hard about what has genuinely given you a real sense of achievement. And try not to use examples that are always related to a work situation.

Many job application forms and online applications also ask about achievements, so it's worth putting in time considering yours.

Be really aware of your achievements.

Many candidates dread questions about achievements. Make the best possible impression by listing them now. It may even be worth talking them through with a friend or colleague; this sometimes helps to get your thoughts going.

When/where	Achievement	What it meant to me
At work		
At school		
At university/college		
Through sport		
Through art, music or drama		
Through voluntary work		
Through other leisure activities		
Through community work or politics		
Through family, friends or other social events		
Any other areas of personal development		

brilliant tip

Be sure to consider all aspects of your experience when you are listing your personal qualities: it is very easy to dismiss some of your own experiences because you are so familiar with them.

Q What is the most interesting thing you have ever done?

A The six months I spent travelling, and especially the time I spent in India, was a completely new and different experience for me and made a lasting impression. As well as learning a lot about a different culture and seeing different sights, I learned to be a lot more observant and a lot more personally resourceful.

Q What are your three greatest strengths?

A Dealing with people, keeping calm when people around me are getting agitated and finding imaginative solutions to problems. Imaginative solutions I have come up with have included using our office space more effectively; I think I have a little bit of a flair for design. I also developed motivation courses for junior staff because we were suffering from a rather high staff turnover.

Q If we asked a friend of yours to describe your character, what would they say?

A I think they would say I am easy to get on with and outgoing. They would say I have a good sense of humour and am generally cheerful. I think they would also say I am good in a crisis – I am often the person who gets telephoned or called on if someone has a problem.

Q If we asked one of your friends to pick out a weakness of yours, what do you think they might say?

Ⓐ I suppose they might say that I can sometimes be a bit impulsive – I get very fired up by a new idea and sometimes a little frustrated if I don't get the chance to carry it through. The plus side of it is that I do have some exciting ideas and many of them do really work.

(Give an example here if this applies to you.)

Ⓠ **What would you say is your most significant fault?**

Ⓐ Getting involved in other people's work. Because I do have considerable experience, colleagues quite often come to me for advice and I am happy to give it; but I have had to learn, and I really have addressed this issue, that it is still their responsibility, I mustn't try to take over. It stems from wanting to be helpful and wanting to see things done well, I suppose.

Ⓠ **How do you cope with disappointment?**

Ⓐ Of course, I don't like it, but I have learned to be philosophical. I was really disappointed when I didn't get into my first-choice university and yet I ended up enjoying myself and doing well. There is a real difference between disappointments that are beyond your own control and those where you can learn something and try to improve your situation. My disappointment over university made me start applying early to the companies that interested me so that I could avoid disappointment.

Ⓠ **You say you are a 'people person': what do you understand by this?**

(They have noticed you resorting to a cliché, now is the time to redeem yourself).

Ⓐ I mean I like being in an environment with plenty of opportunities to discuss ideas with other people and test out my ideas on them. In my current job there are five other people in my team and we are all motivated: our current project has been really successful.

Q Can you say 'no'?

A If I think I have been asked to do something that is really beyond my responsibility or remit, or if I could do it but not within the time-frame that is expected, then I will say 'no'. It is better than agreeing to do something and then finding that you can't deliver or that you have to spend time renegotiating or getting behind with other work. People who have worked with me in the past have acknowledged that I only say 'no' when I really do have a good reason, not just to avoid work or to be unhelpful. I am always open to discussing something and trying to help find a resolution to a situation, though.

brilliant tip

Don't be disconcerted by this question. It provides a golden opportunity for you to highlight your assertiveness skills. You imagine the interviewer wonders whether you are dogmatic, unhelpful and lazy, or whether you are a doormat that can be pushed around by everyone. The question often comes up when you are being asked about time management, assertiveness or communications in general. What you need to tell interviewers is that you can be firm and say 'no' when it is important and reasonable to do so.

Sounds very interesting

Applicants for jobs often ask why they should have to spend time on their application forms, CVs and at interviews describing their leisure activities, pastimes and interests. Candidates often worry that they don't have any sporting or outlandish interests (believing that these are the ones of which employers are most likely to approve). Like many others, this is one of those interview topics that gets you wondering what your rival candidates have been up to that could thrill and impress.

It is also true that how much attention is paid to your leisure activities in an interview will depend on the stage of your career you have reached. If you have a lengthy work history to talk about, interests may take a back seat. If you are a school leaver, they may form a very important part of the interview.

brilliant tip

If your favourite pastime is Morris dancing or playing with your iPhone it is probably best to keep this to yourself. Some interests are best treated as a private matter. (Sorry, Morris dancers everywhere.)

There are several reasons why interviewers want to know about your interests. If there is something you really enjoy doing and are passionate about, they can see you at your most enthusiastic and relaxed self and find out what you are really like when you are keen on something. It is their hope that this infectious enthusiasm will be a characteristic that you can bring to your job. They may also be trying to find out something about your time management skills – are you able to fit anything else in besides work, study and family? You may have interests that have developed skills that are very beneficial to your work situation. If you have been involved in team sports or other group activities, this will be one way in which you have developed awareness of how groups of people function together. If you are involved in the performing arts, you are likely to be confident in a public situation. There are some jobs where having the confidence to take calculated risks is essential and, if your interests reflect a thirst for adventure, this will be a bonus (provided you don't break your leg a week after joining the company in your drive to become an international snowboarding champion).

More than all these reasons, though, what we choose to do in our free time can speak volumes about what kind of people we are, be that extrovert, sociable, persistent, solitary, creative, energetic, cautious, daring, etc. Don't use jargon and terms specific to your interest that others might not understand.

Q Are you easy to get along with?

(Not that anyone is likely to answer 'no'.)

A I really enjoy working with other people and I don't find myself getting into confrontations. If I think trouble is brewing, I am likely to mention it pleasantly at an early stage. I managed to get a colleague who was always late to get to work on time by making a joke of it. I was not the manager, so I could not pull rank, but my method worked.

brilliant tip

'Show don't tell' is what movie actors are told. In the context of the interview, always try to give an example to back up what you have just said.

Q You have talked about your current and past jobs and what you got out of education, but you haven't said much about your interests. How do you spend your leisure time?

A I would certainly say I was a very sociable person; I enjoy company and like entertaining or relaxing with friends. I suppose I have a pretty broad range of interests rather than one overriding passion, but I enjoy music of many different kinds – I play a little bit of guitar, though nothing brilliant. I enjoy reading, especially modern fiction, and I take an interest in current affairs, especially those that affect my own local community, for example the plans to close down our local swimming pool.

Q You say you read a lot of non-fiction as well as fiction. What is the latest non-fiction work you have read and how would you recommend it, or not, to others?

A Ben Goldacre's *Bad Science* – I'm really interested in science, and it made me think much more critically and be more sceptical about articles that I read on the Internet. It was also very entertaining. I would certainly recommend it, even if you are not that interested in science; I think it could awaken interest and awareness.

brilliant tip

Just because interests might seem like a 'soft' topic, don't be tempted to lie. Your interviewer really may be an avid reader, virtual games player, opera buff or keen golfer, so don't bluff and get caught out.

Q I see that you play for your local football team. What sort of a player are you?

(They are probably more interested in your team skills than whether you are a hot goal scorer.)

A I usually play at least once a week and I suppose I'm one of the better players. I captain the team when our usual captain is away and I like to encourage young players.

Q I see you are interested in amateur dramatics. Do you think this will be useful to you at work?

A Well, it has certainly given me a lot of confidence. I used to worry about public speaking, whereas now I really enjoy it. For instance, when giving presentations to small groups, I find I am quite good at holding my audience's attention and I have learned to use visual aids sparingly, rather than relying on them.

Q **I notice that you are chair of your local tenants' group. How much work does that involve?**

A Apart from monthly meetings, which I chair, we are involved in meetings with the local council and other community groups to work towards improving the quality of life on the estate – less litter, better street lighting, more activities for young people, etc. I was reluctant to take on the chair at first, but it is a role I have really got into now. More than the actual chairing of the meetings, I enjoy playing a leading part in some of the negotiations we are undertaking with the local council, and we have already had a successful result – the street lighting is much better than it was six months ago.

brilliant tip

Talking about your interests presents you with a fantastic opportunity to impress. Try to use your interests to draw in other information about your personal skills, whether these be in dealing with people, working in teams, organising events or keeping track of expenditure. These are all useful work skills.

Q **Looking at your CV, your interests appear rather solitary: hill-walking, reading, etc. How do you think this reflects your personality?**

(Do they suspect you of being a sad and lonely character, incapable of relating to the rest of the human race?)

A I like to think they suggest a sense of balance. In my current post I spend a lot of time out meeting potential customers, and in the office we are a busy team of ten. I enjoy socialising, but it can be good to relax completely sometimes and do something different. In any case, hill-walking is something I quite often do in company.

Q If you were to take up a new interest, what would it be?

A I have always liked the idea of sailing. I love swimming and the water and I like the idea of the challenge, having to think and plan according to weather and tides as well as the physical activity. It was my New Year's resolution to start this year and, as it is only February, I am determined to make it a reality.

Q What are your interests outside work?

A I enjoy reading, music, films, theatre, most sports, travel, cooking, gardening and much more.

Q What would you do if you did not have to work for a living and had unlimited leisure time?

A It's hard to imagine. It's something everyone says they would like, but when it came to it, it would probably be more difficult. I would certainly spend more time improving my piano playing and I would like to learn a foreign language – I regretted dropping languages at school. I think I would have to become involved quite heavily in some voluntary community work, though, rather than doing things for myself all the time.

---

brilliant tip

Simply listing loads of different activities does not create the right impression. Avoid listing interests with no explanation of any of them, and don't list so many that your interviewer is left wondering how you manage to squeeze a working day into this busy life. Karl Marx might have said that the fulfilled human being participates in at least five different meaningful activities every day, but it is a rare employer indeed who relishes an introduction to Marxist theory halfway through a job interview.

Take care not to get carried away when you are talking about something that interests you. It is easy to fall into this trap because for you it is 'safe' territory. Restrict yourself to aspects of your interests that say something about you, rather than giving your interviewer a lecture on the rules of contract bridge or advice on exactly which alpine to plant in their rockery. What is a passion for you could be dull for your interviewer.

Employ your interests to your best advantage. Use the chart below to help you consider how your interests describe your personality. Use this information to strengthen your answers during interviews.

Interest/leisure activity	What it says about me

brilliant tip

Whatever activity you are describing and whether it relates to work or leisure, consider the following list of active verbs and try to draw some of them into your answers. Do this now, and thinking in this way will become second nature – you won't have to do it for every interview.

Achieve	Identify	Perform
Analyse	Implement	Persuade
Arrange	Initiate	Plan

▶

Calculate	Interact	Produce
Communicate	Mediate	Select
Create	Modify	Simplify
Decide	Motivate	Succeed
Develop	Negotiate	Test
Establish	Organise	

Don't drive yourself to distraction trying to remember which ones you have included in your answers so far.

Multi-skilled for a changing world

Chapter 3 gave examples of many of the questions you are likely to face relating to your past and current employment and some of these questions asked for particular qualities and skills that your work has developed – managing your time, coping with pressure, etc. Some interviewers will ask these types of question, not necessarily in relation to your employment but to give you the freedom to illustrate these qualities with the best examples you can give from all your life experiences. This is particularly useful for people who have not been in the employment market for very long and is essential for those entering it for the first time.

Q How good are you at dealing with people?

A It is something I really enjoy. I like contact with colleagues and clients and would generally describe myself as a sociable person. I am good at getting the level of my communication right; it doesn't matter whether it is the finance director or someone who has come to fix the computer system.

(If you have encountered an exceptionally mean interviewer, you might get a response such as the following.)

Q **So you spend a great deal of your time talking. Does this leave you time to get on with the job you are supposed to be doing?**

A I know, I did make it sound rather like that didn't I? No, I take my responsibility for running the customer accounts section very seriously, but I have found that when you are chasing customers for money, you often get on better by being pleasant than by becoming the kind of person whose telephone calls they want to ignore.

Q **How good are your writing skills?**

A My main strength is that my writing skills are adaptable. Through my course I developed academic writing skills, but they are obviously not what are required in business situations. I have been secretary for a local social club for a year or two, which means I am good at taking notes and also writing basic business correspondence. I don't just rely on the spell-checker on my computer, I'm quite happy to use a dictionary.

A My business studies course at school meant we had to write business letters of various kinds and I always got good marks for those and for my English assignments. I am already the one in our family who ends up writing official letters if anyone needs to write them – actually it's something I really enjoy.

Q **What level and range of ICT skills do you have?**

A I am quick and efficient with Word and Excel. I am more used to a PC, but I have spent a bit of time using Macs. Of course all the data systems at work are on computer; but I have a home computer, and keeping up with helping my children with their homework really got me interested, so I did an evening course 18 months ago.

Q What do you use your home computer for?

(They are not expecting to find out about your shopping list, or worse.)

A I have always been interested in photography, so I have been getting quite familiar with Photoshop: it has been great for keeping in touch with family members living in other parts of the world. I also help produce a newsletter for our local sports club.

Q Give me an example of your negotiating skills.

A I recently persuaded various local shops and small businesses to take out paid advertising space in a programme for a fund-raising day in aid of our community sports centre. It was really hard at first. People weren't out-and-out unwilling, but they were often quite disinterested and had to be nudged several times before they would come up with any money. I got good at being pushy without upsetting people. We raised more than £3,000 in the end.

A It sounds like a small thing, but I share a house with three other people and persuading people to do their share of the cleaning, tidying and maintenance has really been an uphill struggle, especially when people are really resistant. I have developed a combination of being assertive, firm and appreciative as soon as anyone helps out, and it seems to be working.

Q Tell me something about your financial management skills.

A I was always quite good at basic arithmetic and I find it easy to manage my own budget – though obviously I wish it were a larger one I had to manage. I was treasurer for our local church fête last year, and I maintained all the records in Excel as well as presenting the final figures to the committee.

Q How good are your numeracy skills?

A I feel quite happy working with numbers, although I would not want to do it all the time. I can certainly make sense of spreadsheets: for example, I can examine my department's budget and understand it. I have often presented annual reports for my department where quite a lot of information is given as statistics, and I have never had any problem with this. How much time would you anticipate I would be working with figures in this particular post? Your advert mentioned that a reasonable facility with figures would be useful, so I would certainly expect it to form part of the job.

(If there is something you need to clarify, then it is perfectly fine to ask for this clarification at the end of a question. If a question is important to you, you don't always have to save it to the end. Just make sure your questioning is neither too fierce nor too anxious.)

Q What are you like at speaking to a group of people, giving a presentation to a small or fairly large group?

A I have been used to it ever since my student days. We had to present papers in seminars regularly and in all my jobs I have had to give presentations to groups of clients. At first, I found the larger groups more difficult, but I find that as long as I plan what I am going to say carefully, make sure I have good visual aids and stick to an agreed time limit, it goes well – I prefer smaller groups, but that is because there is a greater opportunity for audience participation, discussion, etc.

Q Describe an occasion when you have had to be diplomatic.

A It was actually a work situation and one member of staff was always complaining, to the extent that she got on everybody's nerves, but she was also incredibly sensitive and she was good at her job. I was not her manager, so it was not a case of using authority. I did have to be as tactful as I could, but I began by asking her how she thought her actions might affect others and we took it from there.

Q What is the most recent skill you have acquired?

A I have done a short course in Spanish because we have a lot of dealings with Spanish-speaking countries. I could not say I am fluent, but it has increased my confidence and given me a taste to learn more.

A Last year I was treasurer for our local parent–teacher's association. I felt very daunted because I have never seen myself as a 'numbers' person. Actually, I have discovered that I am really logical and efficient and I have taught myself to set up databases and spreadsheets.

A Thai cookery. I have to confess to not eating particularly well when I was a student, but recently I have become rather a good cook. I love sourcing unusual ingredients and all the planning that goes into entertaining.

Q Have you ever done anything entrepreneurial?

A When I was a student I had been doing one or two dog-walking jobs and thought there might be other animal-care needs out there. I leafleted the area, offering holiday services looking after cats, fish ponds, rabbits, etc. It was quite successful and fitted in well with the summer holidays. Because I had already done the dog-walking, it was easy to get good personal references.

brilliant tip

Candidates attending interviews or preparing CVs often ask what they should do about mentioning skills and interests that might be linked to political parties or religious groups. They are aware that this might sometimes be inappropriate or too personal, but for many job applicants it is a way in which they have developed considerable expertise, gained in confidence and acquired new skills. All you can really do is use common sense – if you are involved in something pretty mainstream, it should not raise hackles or eyebrows; if it is something more fringe, you are probably wiser not to use it. Think about who your employer is too, and work out whether you are likely to elicit antagonism or approval.

When you are thinking about your skills and qualities, whether in the context of work, education, or other aspects of your life, take note of those that are likely to be most relevant to the job for which you are being interviewed.

Here are some examples of how different qualities might apply to different jobs.

- The ability to listen and to be empathetic is important for a personal counsellor.
- Having a cool nerve and a refined sense of judgement are essential if you are conducting large financial transactions.
- Being creative and imaginative is vital if you are designing a book cover.

You can work out those skills and qualities that apply in your case.

Talking about yourself, whether it is your interests, your achievements or your personality, ought to be an enjoyable experience. If you find yourself in social situations where people want to find out more about you, you take it as a compliment, so allow this pleasant reaction to permeate interview conversations too. Describing yourself feels like hard work, but talking about anything that you have enjoyed, whether it relates to work, home or leisure, can give you the chance to appear at your most vivacious, communicative and relaxed.

Summary and reminders

Be prepared to promote your personality while keeping hold of your integrity.

1   Be honest with yourself but kind to yourself.

2   Discuss your strengths and weaknesses with friends and colleagues.

3   When considering interests, be as inclusive as you can. Interests are not just defined leisure activities, they may relate to your work, e.g. information technology; your home, e.g. entertaining or garden design; or your community involvement, e.g. member of the PTA.

4   Relate all your activities and skills to the job for which you are applying.

CHAPTER 6

Choice, change and chance

Your career decisions: how did you take them, why did you make them?

The place you occupy, or would like to occupy, in the whirling world of work could be as a result of scrupulous planning, early certainty and ambition unswervingly pursued, luck, coincidence or serendipity – perhaps a combination of all of these. There are many psychological theories explaining the process of career choice and career decisions but we are, for the most part, unaware of these as we make the journey through school, college and employment to reach the point where we are at present. We know that we thought about various options, talked to people and observed images of various jobs and professions through books, television and films. We experience contact with many jobs first-hand: teachers, doctors, sales staff, plumbers, lawyers, volcanologists (well, not many of us). With all this information, we rarely analyse exactly how we took a career decision and why. Then, we realise that we could be asked about this at an interview and the analysis begins.

brilliant tip

In some situations you can anticipate questions about your career decisions. Make sure you can give well-thought-out answers on your decisions, whichever of the following applies to you:

● You have just left school, college or university and this is your first job.

▶

- You are applying to join a profession for the first time and your training will be expensive for your employer.
- You are making a radical change of career.
- You have been out of the workforce for some time.
- Your qualifications and experience don't seem to fit with the position you are applying for.

Your CV or application form will tell the interviewer about, and remind you of the factual aspects of, your career history: what you did and when you did it. You should turn your attention to the psychology that underpins it. Your motivations, your decisions, your choices and your perceptions could all be up for scrutiny as part of your interview. As was mentioned in the introduction to this book, it is not possible to go through all the career choices and infinite combinations of possible changes of direction, but the following questions and answers illustrate how this topic is likely to be raised at an interview and the answers outline some suitable responses. These questions and answers are easily adapted to match your own situation.

brilliant example

Get started by considering this sample question and answer. The question and answer are followed by a quick analysis of what makes that answer a success.

Q **What do you think is the difference between a career and a job?**

A To me, having a career rather than a job means doing something where there is a chance to progress and to develop. I am not saying there is one set predictable path, but to me teaching is not just a job. I am interested in taking on increased levels of responsibility and in having more of an input into the way the school works with its local community, how we involve more parents and local businesses and how we try to keep a stable, happy group of teachers. I see this post as head of the sixth form as very much part of career development, not just a change of job. To me, a career is something that puts real meaning into your life, rather than just paying your bills for you at the end of the month.

Why this answer works:

● For most professional-level jobs in all employment sectors, interviewers will hope that you see the post you have applied for as part of career development rather than just a job.

● This answer concentrates on the more important issue of what a career means.

● It takes the opportunity to draw in a few of the issues the interviewee cares about. This is especially useful if there has been no chance for this in other parts of the interview.

● It ends on a positive personal note.

Try analysing some of the answers that follow in this chapter to see why they work. You can use the same technique when you are devising your own model answers.

Ⓠ You say you know a job in advertising is right for you. Why?

Ⓐ When I was still at school one of my projects involved helping design programmes for a fund-raising day for the school and I got very interested in the look of the programme and what would make people want to buy it. After that, I managed to get a few days' work experience with an ad agency and that showed me how much more there is to it behind the scenes before an ad ever appears on TV, in a magazine, or on a poster. Most of my employment has been in sales, but always with a view to getting into advertising and capitalising on the communication skills the sales jobs have developed. I am fascinated by what makes customers (including me) choose particular brands; what are the selling points that people go for?

Q What has been the strongest influence on your career decisions?

A I really wanted to be able to apply some of the scientific research skills I had acquired in my course, but I did a placement in a technical laboratory and it made me realise I also wanted to work more directly with people. Being able to combine those two factors has been a strong influence on my decisions. Environmental health draws on all my interests as well as my strengths and experience.

A To begin with it was chance. I had never considered a career in sales; it was only because it was the first job I could get that I accepted it. In fact, I might have gone as far as to say that it wasn't for me. Now, I thrive in the environment and love motivating other team members to share my enthusiasm.

brilliant tip

Avoid answers like 'I saw a programme about it on TV and it looked really interesting', 'I've always been fascinated by the idea of cementation engineering' or, 'I don't really know'. Of course, it is fine to be fascinated by something, but you really need a reason why and a slightly more lengthy explanation as to the source of this fascination.

Q Why do you want to go to medical school?

A I suppose to begin with it was something of a fantasy career, something I had always said I would do. Actually, all through school I was very strong on the sciences, but interested in people and social issues too and, more and more, medicine has begun to seem like a really suitable choice for me and one that I feel highly committed to. I have done some voluntary work at my local hospital and, although that isn't medical experience, I feel quite comfortable in the hospital environment and enjoy talking to patients.

Ⓠ How do you think you would handle the stress, the emotional side of the work, dealing with people who are very ill or dying, breaking bad news to them?

Ⓐ I know that would be difficult and that I haven't yet been tested in those types of situation, but I know just from my own limited experience of being a patient with minor complaints how being listened to and having things explained carefully helps. I hope that during my training I would learn to cope better and better with painful situations, without losing an attitude of caring about patients and being interested in them as people. I would really like to be able to use the fact that I am strong on sciences in a socially worthwhile context.

Ⓠ You say you are interested in a career in investment management. Explain your understanding of what investment management entails.

Ⓐ My understanding is that I would be managing funds for corporate and private clients, researching the performance of particular funds and reporting on those funds. I know that as well as my report-writing and research skills I would have to be decisive, knowing when to buy, when to sell and when to just stay put for the time being. I like taking decisions; I do weigh up pros and cons, but I do it quickly, even if it is a simple thing like choosing a holiday destination or a car.

Ⓠ How did you reach your decision to become an occupational therapist?

Ⓐ For some time I had been considering a career in medicine, and at school I was not aware of much beyond nursing or becoming a doctor. Then through visiting a relative in hospital I came into contact with physiotherapy and occupational therapy and began to look at the two carefully, talking to people in both professions. I like the amount of community work, home visits and the chance to support patients in so many aspects of their lives that occupational therapy provides. I love working with different people; it is a profession where I think I would be very happy and where I could give a lot.

Q What skills do you think a teacher needs?

A To enjoy working with young people and to have an infectious love of their own subject. I remember from my own time at school how easy it was to tell whether a teacher really enjoyed what they were teaching, and I certainly learned much better when they did. I don't think there is just one personality type who is successful, but you need to be a strong person, assertive and fair without being a bully. Respecting your students is important too. I have done a fair bit of community work with teenagers and I find my sense of humour goes a long way in building up good relationships.

(Obviously you can substitute whichever career or training course fits you for this last and many similar question.)

Q Have your career aspirations changed much over the years?

A They have certainly developed and become more ambitious. When I was at school I had a vague idea that I wanted to do something connected with business, even though at the time it was a fairly nebulous concept to me. My business studies degree and my two years with my current company have refined my interests and I am strongly drawn to corporate finance. I am a good communicator, especially when it comes to handling negotiations – I worked with the mergers team for my current employer.

brilliant tip

Take advantage of questions that prompt you to provide seemingly factual information, such as 'What is involved in ...' 'What are essential skills for ...'. Use the opportunity to blend in a positive comment about yourself, as in many of the answers here.

How do you stay well informed and up to date on what is happening in your field?

(Here are two alternative answers because not everyone will be quite as perfect as our first candidate here.)

I am an active member of my professional association; I was area secretary the year before last. As well as attending meetings and seminars I have run some training sessions myself. It's a real incentive to keep current if you are going to start imparting information to other people. I enjoy my profession; I see it as an interest as well as a career, so reading and discussing developments and issues is never a chore.

I always read relevant articles in the press – well, on the Internet now – and the Internet is a great way to keep informed about what competitors are doing.

Have you taken advantage of any staff development or training activities over the past 12 months?

I have attended several conferences on long-term care to keep myself up to date with issues in the sector and I have also been on a team-building course, as well as two customer-care courses. I try to take advantage of courses and conferences when they are on offer; you learn so much from networking as well as from the events themselves.

Q What training needs, if any, do you have at the moment?

A I feel really comfortable about taking on this job straight away, but I am delighted to see that you run staff induction programmes – it always helps to get a quick overview of everything that is going on. Longer term, I would be interested in marketing training – I have seen some excellent short courses advertised.

Nightmare to avoid

One candidate applying for a post as a dental therapist said she would like training in self-defence, stress management and t'ai chi. She was not offered the position.

Q How would you recommend your profession to someone who is considering joining?

A I still find lecturing extremely satisfying, always dealing with new groups of students, human nature coming up with an infinite variety, and I like my subject. I would have to warn anyone considering entering it now that it is very competitive and hard to get a permanent contract, so they would have to be resilient as well as enthusiastic.

Q How do you think your profession has changed since you first joined?

A The effect of technology has to be the most significant thing. It has made some tasks so much easier and given me skills I never expected to acquire. It has also meant doing a great deal more of my own administration. In the end, though, building up good relationships with clients is what counts and I believe that will always be a fundamental part of this work.

Q How do you think this type of work will change in the future?

A I know the Internet is already really significant, but I am quite sure it will become even more so, especially as a way of making direct contact with current and potential customers. I know people talk about 'the paperless office' and it never seems to happen, but I think with a customer base like ours, we are heading that way.

brilliant tip

Use this questionnaire to help organise material to help you answer questions about your career choices and decisions. This exercise is helpful whether you are explaining your current career position or planning a change of direction.

Describe any influences that helped you reach your career decisions:

- Family influences, e.g. jobs you became aware of through family members.
- Influences from your education, e.g. ideas triggered by courses or subjects you studied or projects you undertook.
- Influences through work experience, e.g. part-time jobs, holiday jobs, periods of employment before the one you are currently in.
- Influences through leisure interests, e.g. artistic/creative/ cultural interests or new skills, such as information technology, foreign languages.
- Influences through voluntary work or community activity.
- Changes influenced by your own perceptions and your personal development.
- Influences through planned information research about particular jobs, industries, professions, courses, etc.

If you are making a move within your current profession, you may find it useful to write a job description or a person specification as if you were doing the recruiting. You know which qualities in your own colleagues you find useful, desirable, irritating or unacceptable, so try thinking from the interviewer's point of view.

A change of direction

Changing direction on your career path may arise from your own choices and preferences, or it may be forced upon you through circumstances beyond your control. Whatever lies behind your career change, you will have to ask yourself many of the questions that potential employers will ask you. If you are changing direction because *you* want to, ask why you want to make such a move. It may mean that you have had to take a step down the career ladder to make a move. Perhaps you have taken a career break for a while to return to education or training, to raise a family or to care for a relative or friend. The searching questions that you will have asked yourself and the decision process that you went through to bring about a change of course will be subject matter for any interviewer as you work your way into your newly chosen career.

When you are called for interview, your new employer will want to reassure him- or herself that not only do you have appropriate skills, experience and personal qualities to fit in and do the job, but also you are sure about the direction in which you are now heading. You will face all the usual questions about education, interests, work experience, strengths and weaknesses but, in addition, you will need to have some good answers for questions specifically exploring your change of direction.

Ⓠ **Tell me why you chose to go to university after you had been working in retailing for 15 years.**

(A) Most of all, because I wanted to. At the back of my mind I had always regretted not staying on at school and continuing with my education. I had been successful in my retail career; I started as a junior assistant and I was manager of a large branch before I went back into education. I also believed it would help me make the break into another business and move away from the retail trade.

(Q) **How difficult did you find it returning to education as a mature student?**

(A) It was hard at first and I certainly missed the salary. I had the idea that most of the course would be full of young students who had just left school but, as it turned out, there was a very broad mix on my course. I found a lot of my work and life experience was relevant to issues that we discussed on the course, and I was often able to give real examples of situations, rather than relying on textbook answers.

(Q) **Before you did your degree, you were working as a nurse and now you are applying for work in management consultancy. How do you explain such a change of direction?**

(A) I don't regret the seven years I spent in nursing, but I believe I made a career decision before I was ready and as the result of considerable family pressure. My years in nursing have not been wasted. I developed excellent interpersonal skills, coped with stress and worked well under pressure; I also acquired good administrative skills and experience in training and managing other staff. There are so many problems to be solved when you are dealing with people and their health, and I am sure seeing your way to the heart of a problem is something that will be immensely useful to me in management consultancy. I think my calm attitude and common-sense approach would go down well with clients.

Q **Journalism is extremely competitive. Your background in engineering is, to say the least, unusual, so what makes you think you could succeed in this profession?**

A Before I trained as an engineer I had considered technical journalism as an option. I always did well in English as well as the technical subjects at school, but I was very drawn to designing and producing something tangible rather than talking about it. As I have progressed at work I have looked far more at the trade press and often thought I could write a more read-able article than some of the material I have come across. I have had articles published in a motorcycle magazine and several of my letters have appeared in the local press and occasionally the national press. My CV outlines my IT skills and I know how important they are in journalism today.

Nightmare to avoid

By all means be as creative as you can in making links from past career to present choice, but remember that it can be stretched too far. One candidate being interviewed to join the Royal Air Force said he was applying because he wanted to be an astronaut and the air force was the next best thing. Asked what his relevant experience was to date, he said he had been working on the bacon counter in his local supermarket.

Q **How do we know this change of career direction won't be just a passing phase? You might have another change of heart after we have invested time and money in your training and progress.**

A Well, I believe the fact that I have put so much commitment into making the change is a clear demonstration. Studying for my law exams on a part-time basis was very demanding and I had to be very single-minded about it. My work in housing management meant that I often dealt with people who had legal issues and I gained some familiarity with the court system through the cases we took to court. It is not always easy to make a career decision at 18 that will see you through the rest of your life, but I am quite convinced that the law will hold my interest for at least a couple of decades.

Ⓐ I have used IT a great deal in my current and previous jobs and, although my job description might say 'administrator', I am always the one in the office who troubleshoots if we have problems with the computer side of things, and if I can't solve it I liaise with our technical department. I usually end up training new staff on our systems too. I think I have already made the career change by stealth, but obviously I would like a job where I could develop these skills to a higher level. My interpersonal skills are also good and I think this is a skill that is sometimes neglected by staff working mainly with machines and electronic systems.

Ⓠ **Would you honestly have considered work in this field if you hadn't been made redundant?**

Ⓐ It is true that sales is a new direction for me, but I am very keen and I certainly get on well with people. Being a good supervisor means getting people to do what you want without bullying them and I guess in some ways sales might be similar to that – you want a customer to buy your office supplies, but you want them to feel it's a good decision that they have taken themselves. Having a practical and technical background also means I would be confident demonstrating anything I was selling. I am not saying I was pleased to be made redundant, but a move like this could be good for me and, of course, for my new employer.

Q It sounds as if you are disillusioned with your career in social work/electronics/health and safety. Is there an element of you running away from it rather than actually making a positive choice now?

A I am sure there is an element of that, but that means I have had to think very hard about this change and that I feel really motivated. I am making a carefully reasoned and, I think, wise decision about what I should do next. The skills I have acquired and the qualities I have developed have changed me enormously over the past ten years and I know there are parts of me that are not being used half as effectively as they could be.

(At this point it is important to give a concrete example of an aspect of yourself that you feel your newly chosen career would use, but also emphasise the strengths you already have.)

Q How do you feel about having to start at the bottom again, becoming a trainee, when you have had considerable responsibility in your last job?

A I don't mind at all. I have always been interested in book publishing, in anything to do with books really, and the years I spent in teaching have given me a discerning eye when it comes to spotting a good educational book. I am sure I shall enjoy my training and learn quickly, and I see it as a really exciting opportunity.

Q Because of your limited experience in this field, we couldn't pay you what you are being paid in your current accountancy job. How will you handle taking a drop in salary?

A Well, at least my accounting experience means I am good at making the best of any budget and, of course, I looked very carefully at the financial implications of my decision. I hope my contribution to the company will mean my salary is reviewed in the not too distant future, but I can definitely accept the job on what you are currently able to offer.

Q **How do you deal with change in general?**

A I am quite used to it. There were many changes caused by external factors in my previous job and I think it is really a case of learning not to see it as a threat, but as a chance to look at new ways of doing things. When my last department was amalgamated with another section there were all kinds of anxieties about how we would lose specialist knowledge and expertise, but we ended up all becoming more well informed and more able to help clients effectively.

Q **If you were starting your career all over again, what would you do differently?**

A I am very happy with the way my career has turned out, and my current job in the legal department is a position where I find almost all aspects of my work interesting and enjoyable. I suppose that if I were starting out all over again I might choose to commit to a career connected with commercial law earlier than I did. It was hard work taking extra qualifications part-time. Apart from that, I don't think I would change anything.

brilliant tip

You can make a commanding impression by remaining undaunted by hostile-sounding questions. Your calm and open manner will speak volumes. These questions address real concerns that the interviewer has and are designed, once again, to test your commitment.

It is important to be candid and open about your decision, without feeling obliged to give away private information that is none of your employer's business. You don't have to pretend that you have always had a secret desire to be a train driver, tight-rope walker or whatever else you are moving into. You do have to be clear on what your reasons are and very convincing about your staying power and commitment.

Q **You have never worked for a small business before; give me three reasons why I should offer you the job.**

A I have plenty of ideas about how you could develop your export base; I love working with people and I am sure I could help you be more profitable.

Q **You have worked in local government up until now; do you expect things to be different in this private engineering company?**

A I enjoyed my design work and I was always working to tight deadlines and working within strict budgets, but I do expect a bit less paper work and more time to put into the design side of things. I think if you are part of a good and motivated team, which I was, that is actually more important than which sector you are working in.

In some ways, all this emphasis on explaining career choice and career decisions is surprising. We inhabit a world where the nature of employment has changed and is still changing in this new century. We are frequently told not to expect the notion of a continuous and smoothly progressing career. Economic circumstances, technological change and global markets all contribute to the need to be highly adaptable and flexible in your approach to work – indeed, these are exactly the skills most interviewers claim to be seeking. It is one of the many burdens of being an interviewee that you are arguing a case for your capacity to cope with change when, a few minutes earlier, you were persuading the interviewer that you are a creature capable of planning, organising and anticipating.

Summary and reminders

Remind yourself of the following when you are asked to explain career choice and career change.

1 Review your past to analyse where you are now.

2 Consider the key skills you need to do your current job.

3 Think about the satisfactions and frustrations associated with that job.

4 Ask yourself how you would sell your chosen career to somebody else.

5 If you are planning a change of direction, list the main reasons why.

CHAPTER 7

Climbing the ladder

Show them you are the right person for this job and that you are ready to climb the career ladder if you want to

What role do ambition, drive, career progress and career success play in your life and how would you even begin to define some of those terms as they fit your circumstances? The reason prospective employers are so interested in these aspects of you is that they link to something very important to all employers – your level of motivation: that all-important question 'Will you do the job?' Assuming you have the qualifications, the right experience, an attractive CV and a pleasant interview manner, your interviewer needs to be able to recognise real commitment. Do you really, really want the job – not the job offer and the chance to turn up three weeks on Monday, but the chance to do the work, meet the customers, fit in with the team, contribute to profits, status and quality, to the organisation's future?

What motivates each of us is different; material reward, public acclaim, artistic achievement, intellectual stimulation, contributing to the good of society or feeling morally and ethically at ease are just some of the satisfactions work can provide. Simply finding work a reasonably pleasant place to be so you can go home at the end of the day with a clear conscience and enjoy a good bottle of wine or relaxing cup of tea and an untroubled sleep is the main goal for many people. Finding something that provides all these is, admittedly, rather more of a challenge.

Prepare for your promotion interviews by considering your work values

Before you reach the job interview stage you will have started to consider what matters to you as your career progresses. What is it about work that most gets you up in the morning and stops you dreading Mondays?

Use the following exercise to help you organise this information clearly.

Look at the work values listed here and think about which of them is most important to you. You may wish to add others that are not featured on this list.

- I have been able to get ahead in my chosen career.
- I can help people cope better with their lives – their circumstances.
- The financial rewards are significant.
- I can enjoy at least some degree of job security.
- I have the opportunity to work on my own.
- My work involves some risks, not necessarily physical; they could be financial risks or taking potentially risky decisions.
- There may be opportunities to travel.
- The social status attached to the job is very high.
- There is an opportunity to be creative or inventive.
- I perceive the work as socially useful and of value to society.
- I am given plenty of autonomy in how I manage my own workload.
- There are opportunities to work as part of a team.
- There are opportunities to work with other people, customers, clients or other professionals.
- There is a busy, high-pressure atmosphere.
- There is not too much stress involved.

- There are opportunities to use specific skills, such as information technology, foreign languages and design skills.
- There are plenty of opportunities to train and motivate others.
- There is considerable responsibility at an early stage in my career.
- There are opportunities for further professional training.
- There are opportunities to use interpersonal skills: persuading, negotiating, etc.
- My ideas can make a real contribution to the way work is carried out.
- There is considerable variety in the daily/weekly/monthly tasks I undertake.
- I have the opportunity to use good writing skills.
- I have the opportunity to use mathematical skills.
- Pay is related to performance.
- There are plenty of opportunities for promotion.

It is likely that you are driven by a combination of many of the different factors above and that you are already involved in, or looking for, work that to some extent already matches this profile. If you are clear about what motivates you, it will help you to answer some of the questions that interviewers confront you with to check out your motivation and enthusiasm.

brilliant example

Get started by considering this sample question and model answer. The question and answer are followed by a quick analysis of what makes that answer a success.

Q How far do you intend to go with this organisation?

A All my previous research and the impression I have gained today have confirmed my interest and enthusiasm for this job. I do feel that I am at a ▶

point in my career where I would really like to develop with one company, so I would like to go as far as I possibly can. At this stage, I would be very happy if you offered me the post of project manager; I think I could handle this very well for you. I would like to think that, with greater understanding of your company from the inside, I could progress to the most senior levels of management. I don't feel too impatient, though; your current projects look demanding and interesting.

Why this answer works:

- It starts on a very positive note.
- It is complimentary about the organisation.
- It suggests long-term commitment.
- It provides reassurance that the interviewee is committed to the post on offer.

As an exercise, try constructing an equally positive answer for an interviewee who is keen on the job on offer but content to remain with project management and does not necessarily want to reach the very top.

Try analysing some of the answers that follow in this chapter to see why they work. You can use the same technique when you are devising your own model answers.

How did you get your first job?

A I made applications to all the travel agents that I could reasonably get to without moving home, and the third one that interviewed me offered me a job. I can still remember it so clearly. I knew it was a competitive area to get into and I was really thrilled at getting the chance to do something that interested me.

A I went to talk to someone who was a friend of a friend who was fairly senior in this local small manufacturing company and I was offered a job. I wasn't even sure if I wanted it at that stage, but I was certainly glad of the offer.

Ⓐ I qualified just as we went into a recession, so I had to make a lot of applications, send off dozens of CVs and make what felt like hundreds of telephone calls, though it probably wasn't that many. Eventually I got into a local law firm by offering to do some voluntary work, just photocopying, taking over on reception, that sort of thing, but they ended up taking me on and putting me through the rest of my qualifications.

Ⓠ **How did you get your current job?**

Ⓐ I was approached by a recruitment consultant who was looking for someone to head up a division being created by my current employer. I faced quite a difficult decision because I had enjoyed my previous job and the company had treated me well but, in the end, this was a new challenge, and a financially rewarding one, so I took the decision to make the move. I have been there for three and a half years now and the division is running smoothly, so I feel ready to move on.

Ⓐ As I was making something of a change of direction, from engineering production management to technical authorship, I started applying to any suitable adverts in the national and specialist press as well as approaching some places on spec. In the end, I got my current post through an advert in the trade press.

Ⓠ **Are you looking for a temporary or a permanent job?**

(Obviously your answer – whatever you would really prefer – is going to be influenced by what you know is on offer but, depending on what is on offer, interviewers might be looking for something like one of the following answers.)

Ⓐ As I would be leaving a permanent job, I would really prefer to move into something else permanent, especially something like this where there seem to be real opportunities for me to develop with the organisation. Now that I have passed all my professional exams, I would really like to commit to a company that I like and stay there for the foreseeable future.

Ⓐ I would be quite happy with a temporary post at the moment. I think it would be a good opportunity for me to get a bit more experience in market research. If things worked out well from your point of view and mine, and something permanent were to be on offer in the future, then I would certainly consider applying for it.

Ⓐ I would like to move out of supply teaching and into a permanent post now. I have learned a great deal from working in different schools and I have worked in some that face real problems as well as some that are doing well. Establishing rapport with classes quickly and maintaining discipline is really good experience. Having been round the school today, the atmosphere is really excellent and I would love a permanent post here.

brilliant tip

To create the best possible impression, make it clear that whether you had a stroke of good luck or faced considerable difficulty when looking for work, you remained active, in control and prepared to take decisions.

Ⓠ **Why have you decided to leave your current job?**

Ⓐ I am still enjoying my work and my last appraisal suggested I am ready to take on more management responsibility, but it seems unlikely that the business will grow for the next year or two – I don't want to get into the position where I am just coasting.

Ⓠ **What could you do to make your job more interesting, then, if you are saying it isn't really challenging you?**

(In other words, whose fault is it that you are coasting; is it you or your employer?)

Ⓐ I have already taken some measures. I have volunteered to take on more responsibility for staff training and I recently initiated a new customer satisfaction survey, but I still feel I could be doing more, especially in managing and motivating larger sales teams.

(Other possible reasons for leaving a job include the following.)

Ⓐ I had anticipated and been told that a major part of my current job would involve redesigning, developing and maintaining the organisation's website – this was what really grabbed me about the job and also what my qualifications and my previous job had prepared me for. I was quite happy to help out with other administrative tasks within the department – I accept that we all need to help out – but administration has ended up taking up about 70 per cent of my time; the website seems to be a low priority and I don't want to lose my skills through lack of use.

Ⓐ I hadn't been planning to leave; it is only when I saw this position advertised that I really felt it was an opportunity not to be missed. I really welcome the idea of being able to use my writing skills as well as my IT skills – they are my major work interests – so I just had to give this one a go.

Whether you are seeking promotion, or a job on a similar level to the one you hold at present, interviewers want to know if you are difficult to work with.

Ⓠ **How do you react if a colleague criticises your work?**

Ⓐ It depends how valid I believe the criticism to be and to some extent how it is put to me, but I do listen to the point being made and try not to be too sensitive. I like to share ideas and suggestions with other people and sometimes what seems like an adverse comment has taught me something very useful.

Q How do you react if a colleague sends you an e-mail which you consider to be discourteous?

A That's interesting, because I think people often are more careless or less considerate when firing off e-mails than when you had to compose a memo. On the whole, though, I try to brush off minor discourtesies while remaining polite myself. If the issue became serious, e.g. harassing or abusive, I would obviously have to take the matter further.

---

brilliant tip

When you are describing your good communication skills, be sure to include e-mail; many people forget that there is a distinction between e-mails to friends and e-mails at work.

Q How do you react if you don't get your way over a work issue?

A It would depend on how crucial I think that issue is to our business. One of our senior managers wanted to bring in changes that would have altered everyone's jobs and responsibilities and I felt that this would actually mean a far less effective service to our clients with a lot of specialist knowledge being lost. I was very against the idea, but I put my arguments down very thoroughly, and I hoped quite persuasively, on paper so that management would have ample opportunity to consider my point of view. To my delight it worked and the plans were shelved. Of course, it does not always work in my favour like that, but I know I can make a persuasive argument when I have to and I can also accept the decisions of others if necessary.

Q When did you last lose your cool at work?

A Not since I was very new and inexperienced. I have learned to be firm without blowing my top and I think it sets a poor example when any staff, but especially senior managers, are out of control.

Ⓐ The day a new computer system failed to do what it had been designed to do. I had had no part in the commissioning, but I was not the only one who was really frustrated. It has taught me to ask lots of questions at a very early stage in any project planning.

Ⓠ **What do you think of your current manager?**

Ⓐ She is very effective, especially at delegating the right tasks to the right people and I have learned a lot from her. If I were to make a criticism it is that I think she could achieve more by involving wider groups of staff in consultation before decisions are made – sometimes she loses goodwill from an otherwise highly motivated staff team.

Ⓠ **What do you think of your current employer?**

Ⓐ As an employer, they are fine and I have no complaints, but I would like to see them being a little more imaginative about the range of fashion clothes we sell. Working on the buying side, it can be frustrating when you feel you have good ideas and there is not really an outlet for them. Of course, you have to accept that not all your ideas will be good ones, but our sales figures were not brilliant for last year, as you know, so we do need to do something.

Ⓠ **How do you maintain your interest in your current job?**

Ⓐ Quite easily. I am working on several accounts each for different clients and so my work has a lot of variety, both on a daily and on a more long-term basis. No two accounts are ever the same even if, in theory, the process that you go through is almost identical.

Nightmare to avoid

A nightmare can be saying that your current boss is the most hideous and evil megalomaniac that ever walked the planet and that you have serious doubts as to whether he is even from this planet and then finding he is a close personal friend of the chair of the interview panel. Careful, measured criticism of your current role/organisation may be OK, but whining is definitely out. Loyalty is a quality that is prized by all employers, so even if you are currently working for a competitor, appearing disloyal will not gain you friends.

Q Tell me about a work target you have set yourself.

A It sounds simple, but a few months ago I decided I would always complete relevant paperwork at the end of the day, even if it made me a bit late. It has made a real difference to my level of energy and I have become far more productive. I am trying to spread this good practice among colleagues now.

A I noticed that some people weren't saying anything at our section meetings, so I decided to make a point of asking everyone something, without making them feel too put on the spot. I set it as my objective to get everyone to contribute. It has worked well, though I think one or two quieter members of the team found it a little daunting at first.

Q What is your current salary?

A At the moment I am paid … though if I remain with my current employer I am expecting an increase in three months' time. Pay rises are linked to annual performance reviews and I have received an increase every year so far.

Ⓐ I currently receive ... but I would hope to better that if I were to be offered a post here.

✦ brilliant tip

Do check what similar posts in similar organisations are worth before committing yourself, then be realistic but optimistic.

Don't be frightened of questions concerning what you expect to be paid. If you ask for too much, the worst that can happen is they can say 'no'. If you ask for too little, they are not likely to try to persuade you to ask for more.

Ⓠ **What salary are you expecting us to pay you?**

Ⓐ My current salary is ... and I do expect to better that when I take up a new post. Looking at your job description I see the job with you as being more demanding and that is one of the reasons I have applied, but I would hope that increased responsibility would be reflected in what you are prepared to pay me.

Ⓐ Having moved from an organisation with a fixed salary structure, I find it is a new experience to be negotiating my own pay, but I have researched what a current reasonable rate for this job would be and I know I am well qualified and keen, so I would expect at least ...

Ⓠ **Do you think being a graduate should affect your starting salary?**

Ⓐ I would like to think so, but I am actually more interested in speedy career progression which would, of course, affect my salary. I think my course is very relevant to this position and I am sure I would enjoy working here.

brilliant tip

While you should never undersell yourself, it is important to be pragmatic and realistic. Getting your foot in the door can sometimes be more important than the level of your starting salary.

Q Do you think you are being paid enough?

A I know that what I am paid equates favourably to others on a similar level in my profession, but I am prepared to put in extra time and extra effort and I believe it is reasonable that I should be rewarded for this.

A Not really. I took on the position at a fairly low salary because at that stage I did not have much direct experience in the field, but I caught up quickly and I have a good track record. I intend to negotiate for more money if I remain in my current situation and I expect a degree of success in my negotiations.

brilliant tip

With the current competition for jobs in this tough economic climate, don't let lack of confidence drag you down when you are talking about money. Be sure that you have considered what is the least you would accept and what you would really like. If this is clear in your own mind, you are far less likely to sound bumbling and vulnerable when you are discussing pay. Remember also that the worst that can happen if you ask for more than they are prepared to pay is that they will say: 'Sorry, no can do.'

Q Where do you see yourself in three years' time?

A As I have only just entered the physiotherapy profession, part of me would like to keep my options open, learn as much as I can and gain from the different specialisms I shall come into contact with over the coming years. I really enjoyed my work on neurology during my training, so that may be a direction I choose. Management does interest me in the longer term, but I want several years of working with patients before I move in that direction.

Ⓐ This is a lively and expanding company by all accounts, and from what I have learned so far I very much hope that I shall still be here in three years' time. I chose to apply for your customer operations division because it seems to me a great way to learn a lot about your services, your customers and your finances. I do, however, have an open mind about moving into other divisions, if this helped me learn more and prepared me more effectively for senior management.

Promoting your cause

Promotion interviews can be demanding. You are not only illustrating how well you work in your current role or profession, but also being asked to demonstrate that you are suitable to take on more, to face new challenges and accept new tasks. To some extent then – whatever evidence you produce – you are being taken partly on trust.

You face many similar questions, however, whether you are seeking promotion with your current employer, or whether you are trying to take a step up the career ladder. In either case, you will have to convince your interviewer of your suitability.

Promoting your own interests

Ⓠ **What do you want out of this promotion?**

Ⓐ Of course, I want the opportunity to take on more responsibility but, specifically, I know that a job at this level will mean more opportunity to contribute to decisions. I like the fact that the job would require me to get involved in strategic planning. My past project-planning experience will prove very useful in this respect.

🅐 I know this job will involve less direct contact with customers, but I think I can serve our customers better by taking responsibility for training other staff in customer care and for developing policies that enhance customer support. I have enjoyed my customer contact and used it to learn about what they see as good service and what really irritates them – I would love the chance to act on this. I can give you some ideas if you like.

Nightmare to avoid

At one particular promotion interview, each candidate had been asked to prepare a brief presentation to put to the panel. Materials were provided for this purpose. One candidate boldly announced that he was not going to use loads of fancy coloured pens and time-wasting charts like the nitwit who preceded him (he had seen what he thought was a previous candidate's handiwork in the preparation room). It turned out to be a chart prepared with time and effort by none other than one of the interview panel for a training meeting session the following day. Not a winning strategy.

🆀 **We have several internal applicants for this post. If we do offer you the job, how would you cope with any possible resentment from these disappointed candidates about an outsider being brought in?**

🅐 Whenever I take up a new job, I try to listen and learn, so that I get a good idea of what the issues, problems and personalities are in the team that I am working with. I would certainly adopt a professional approach to everyone I worked with and, of course, I would hope that other staff would do the same. On the other hand, disappointment can be hard to cope with and if resentment seemed to be affecting the way someone worked, or the way we worked together, then I think I would have to talk to him or her about it and offer reassurance and encouragement. If their behaviour became totally unreasonable, then I might have to consider other approaches.

brilliant tip

You might also have to adapt this answer if you are applying for an internal promotion and other staff from your section or department are rivals for the job. In fact, this can actually be a more difficult situation to deal with if you are successful.

(Q) **You are probably aware that two of your colleagues have applied for this job. If you are successful, how will this affect the way you work?**

(A) It won't, at least not in my attitude to working with them, and I would hope we would all take that approach. If I take on the job I would use the opportunity to ensure that everyone in the department was motivated and getting a chance to take on tasks and responsibilities where they excel. I am sure this would help smooth any ruffled feathers.

(Q) **What new ideas would you bring to the job that other candidates would not?**

(A) I would spend some time getting to know the department, so that I could assess what was already working well, but also see whether there were areas where we could be more efficient. My recent management diploma gave me the opportunity to look closely at how to get the best skills mix in work groups, getting better results for the company and higher job satisfaction among staff members. I see that you do have project groups within the department, so some of my ideas could be very effective here.

Ⓐ I became good at finding creative solutions to problems both logistical and practical when I did two years of voluntary service overseas. Quite often it was impossible to get either the equipment or the personnel that you would ideally have liked, so you just had to work with whatever was available. I was involved in building projects, so obviously we could not compromise on safety, but I certainly learned to be flexible.

Ⓠ **How tough are you if it comes to disciplining a staff member?**

(This question is not exclusive to promotion, but such responsibilities tend to increase as you climb the professional ladder.)

Ⓐ It is a situation I have already had to deal with in my current job where I had a staff member with a very poor time-keeping record. We tried to be flexible because of his domestic situation, but being flexible is very different from allowing someone to take advantage. I would be as firm as was necessary, double-check the rules and regulations and legal situation before I jumped in, but I would also be sure I was being fair. Where necessary I would consult with other appropriate staff.

Ⓠ **You haven't been in your current post very long. Do you think you are ready for this promotion?**

Ⓐ Of course; I feel confident and very excited about the prospect of becoming a deputy head. I may not have been in teaching for that many years, but I came into the profession as a mature person, with considerable work experience behind me. Also, having my own children in school before I started teaching has given me a well-grounded understanding of the issues that face the profession, the changing demands and pressures that we face. I believe I am the kind of leader who draws colleagues with me, rather than one who pushes them from behind.

Q How will you feel if you don't get this promotion?

A Naturally it will be a disappointment – it is something I really want, I feel ready for it and I think I have had plenty of experience in all aspects of the hotel business and this particular hotel. However, I still enjoy my current job as deputy manager so I don't imagine I would immediately become disillusioned and lose interest in my work.

Q Why haven't you applied for something at this level before?

A I did think about it a year or two ago, but there was a project I really wanted to see through to the end and I was still enjoying what I was doing. In fact, I still am, but I really do want to manage a larger team now.

Q This position would make considerable demands on your qualities as a leader. What would you say is your leadership style?

A I am a strong leader and I suppose I would describe myself as a bit of a shaper, good with new ideas and quick to spot how to delegate effectively and take on appropriate work myself. I have learned a lot about my management style from working on joint projects with managers of other departments where I have had to work in a more cooperative way. This has been useful: I am still a strong leader, but I have learned the value of consultation and of making the best use of the skills every team member has.

Q This job looks quite similar to the one you are currently doing – why have you applied for it?

A It is true that your job description looks quite similar to the one I am working to at present, but I really don't believe any two jobs are the same: different customers, different projects and different approaches. I am ambitious, but I believe one of the ways to realise that ambition is to gain a thorough understanding of the business first. I see this move as a very exciting one.

brilliant tip

Don't be put off by questions that appear to be criticising your decisions: you are explaining your decisions not justifying them. It is also possible that they want to check whether you become defensive, so don't play into their hands.

Q What motivates you in your current job?

A I chose to become a healthcare assistant because I believed I would enjoy working with people and I liked the idea of working in a healthcare setting. I did not have many formal qualifications, and my previous work experience had been mostly in retail. In retail, I liked dealing with customers, but I wanted to do something where I worked more closely with people and felt I was helping them. I really enjoy my work; although a lot of the time I am giving physical care, you get to know patients and sometimes have a bit more time to talk to them and make them feel better, whereas some of the professional staff simply don't have time for this. I do like working as part of a team too. I have now taken an NVQ level 2 and in time I would like to take more qualifications.

Q Do you think you are overqualified for this job?

A No, I don't. I think my experience and qualifications will mean that I can do the job very effectively from day one and be a very useful member of the department straight away. I have been keen to work in a smaller company like this ever since I left university. I would enjoy the job and you would get a good new member of staff.

> ### ☀ brilliant tip
>
> Some questions simply cry out for you to make a brilliant impression. Be well prepared for questions where, as they say in the money markets, 'It's time to sell, sell, sell' and the product is you. This applies whether you are seeking promotion, or looking for a change.

Ⓠ We are seeing several candidates today. What makes you stand out from the others?

Ⓐ All my qualifications and experience relate directly to what your job description says you require but, more than that, your plan to expand into Europe ties in very well with my recent spell in Paris. The staff I have met here today and this interview have convinced me that I would fit in extremely well here and would really enjoy it, which is always a great motivator.

Ⓠ Give me the three main reasons why we should give you this job.

Ⓐ As I already manage a health centre with real success I can certainly demonstrate that I can do the job. In addition, I am good at coming up with and acting on new ideas. For example, I developed a scheme where more of our patients could access different complementary therapies and yet this had little effect on our overall budget. Team skills are one of my real strengths. It is so easy, when several groups of professionals are involved, for work situations to become divisive or competitive in an unhelpful way. I am good at fostering understanding and coop-eration between different work groups. On top of those reasons, I am really enthusiastic about this post; I would put a great deal of energy into it.

Q **Would you take this job if we offered it to you?**

A Yes, definitely. I was keen as soon as I saw your advert and your job description fits my skills and experience very well. More than that, actually meeting potential colleagues and finding out more about your current activities has clarified what an exciting challenge it would be to work here.

> **brilliant tip**
>
> Unless you are absolutely certain that you won't want the job under any circumstances, always sound enthusiastic. You are not committed until you have signed a contract.

Is someone after your head?

As you gain more experience in your chosen field it is likely that you may use recruitment agencies or consultants to help you find work. It is also possible that head hunters will seek you out to ascertain your suitability for a particular position. You should work just as hard at your interviews in either of these instances.

Q **Your CV looks good, but we have several people on our books who are just as well qualified – what makes you stand out?**

A I think the fact that I have worked for both a large and a very small firm has given me a really good perspective on getting the best out of people and spotting small problems before they become large ones. I noticed, for example, that several small customers left us when we changed our IT system, so we were quickly able to encourage them back again.

Seeking promotion, or seeking a change – in both cases you must recognise new or different aspects of the work as well as those that are similar to your current or previous positions, so that you are not caught out with comments such as, 'Well, you haven't done anything quite like this before'.

Summary and reminders

As you climb the career ladder, tread carefully and prepare for the next step.

1   Consider what really is important to you about your work.

2   Prepare for questions that focus on your loyalty and your commitment.

3   Link past experience to any new responsibilities and tasks that you are aware will form part of the job you are applying for.

CHAPTER 8

Are you confident that you are competent?

Competence-based or
behaviour interviews – use
them to your advantage

Recruiting the best people is probably the most important task that any employer undertakes, so they try hard to find methods of interviewing that will be effective and will provide accurate predictors of who is likely to make the perfect employee. This has led to an increasing trend in what is referred to as competence-based interviews.

> **brilliant tip**
>
> Be sure you know what competency is. Competency means being able to do something, having the ability to perform a particular task or fulfil a particular function effectively.

Sometimes competency-based interviews are disconcertingly referred to as 'behaviour interviews', but this term is used to cover work competencies rather than etiquette. These interviews do not focus on your education, work history or interests. You won't get asked why you want the job or to tell the interviewer(s) about yourself. These interviews focus on whether you have the right abilities to do a particular job, and do it well.

Interviews based on or including a large element of competency-based questions are becoming very much the norm. You are most likely to encounter them if you are being interviewed for positions in large organisations. Not all interviewers who use them necessarily like them. Some complain that they are inflexible and artificial and that they do not give them such a full picture of the whole person. If you are reading this, however, then your present sympathies are not likely to be with the plight of interview panel members. Your concern is what you can expect from these interviews and how you can ensure that you can tackle them well to optimise your chances of success.

Below is a list of some of the most commonly sought abilities. Don't be put off by the list. No single interviewer is likely to require you to have evidence of everything on the list. Usually, employers have a list of six or seven that are the most relevant to a particular post. Job descriptions and person specifications are likely to tell you what these are, so you should not be taken by surprise.

- Adaptability
- Communication – listening speaking, writing
- Decision-making
- Entrepreneurial flair
- Influencing
- Imagination
- Innovating
- Leadership
- Management of people, resources and projects
- Negotiating and persuading
- Planning
- Problem-solving
- Project management
- Relationship-building
- Resource management
- Self-management
- Strategic thinking

- Teamwork
- Using and developing expertise

You might encounter competence-based interviews at whatever level you are applying and in whatever type of employment. They are popular in many professions, from sales to healthcare, and at all levels of supervisory and management recruitment.

The dividing line between competence-based and other interviews is often blurred. Many employers interview using a combination of biographical, general, scenario and competence questions. In previous chapters, you have already encountered a few competence-type questions. This chapter develops these in more detail.

brilliant tip

Here is a quick way to spot when you are being asked a competence-type question. It will start with a phrase like 'Describe an occasion', 'Outline a situation', 'Tell me about a time', etc., so you are being clearly and openly invited to describe specific and real experiences.

Preparing for competence-based interviews

There is no formula for preparing for these, but there are some points to keep in focus. This book has emphasised frequently the need to prepare plenty of concrete examples, from work, education and other aspects of your life, to illustrate the skills, qualities and potential that you claim to possess when you are being interviewed. The requirement to do this is most important in the competence-based interview. You simply cannot say something vague, like 'I believe I have very good communication skills', in reply to the question 'Give an example of how you have used your communication skills'.

Now for some examples of competence-based questions.

brilliant example

Get started by considering this sample question and model answer. The question and answer are followed by a quick analysis of what makes that answer a success.

Ⓠ Tell me about how you deal with the busiest times in your job and give me an example.

(Your organisational ability is being checked out.)

Ⓐ Each year, the small company I work for runs an awards ceremony for the healthcare sector. Part of my role is to be the main coordinator for this. I have to book the venue, organise the entries and arrange the judging before the awards night. I also organise all the practical side: venue, after-dinner speakers, caterers, etc. There are 20 awards, so it is very hectic. I always work to a checklist when I am planning my time, and I budget some time for last-minute hitches, because there are always a few that are out of our control. I let colleagues know in plenty of time what I need from them, so they aren't under unreasonable pressure. I try to learn something each time round, so that things take less time during the following year. I enjoy the buzz of this part of the year, though. I am sure I could put this experience to good use working on your sales exhibitions.

Why this answer works:

- It offers a very clear example of a piece of work that does demand a lot of organisational ability.
- It breaks down the answer into some of those individual tasks, e.g. organising, catering, judging, etc., rather than relying on a vague 'There is a lot to organise'.
- It demonstrates what you do to be well organised: making lists, planning ahead and informing colleagues.
- It makes it clear that you enjoy being really busy.
- It ends on a positive link from what you have done to what you could do in the new job.

Try analysing some of the answers that follow in this chapter to see why they work. You can use the same technique when you are devising your own model answers.

(Q) How many hours do you expect to work in a week to get the job done?

(Your time management is being checked out here.)

(A) I always plan and prioritise work as much as I can, so I should be able to accomplish as much work as possible in a normal working day and make sure that I meet any targets or deadlines that come up. A busy time for me is just before the annual report has to go to print, because I have to provide a lot of statistics for this and they have to be recent, so even if you think ahead, there is inevitably some last-minute work. I am prepared to put in extra hours at hectic times like this, but I try not to make this a daily habit.

(It is worth knowing a bit about the work culture of the organisation you are applying to when answering questions like this. Do they have an ethos that states that they would like all employees to be off the premises by 5.30 p.m., or do they state that people are expected to put in a great many extra hours regularly? Answers to questions like this help you to work out how you feel about working there, not just how to answer interview questions.)

(Q) How did you get on in the first week the last time you took up a new job?

(You are being asked just how adaptable you really are.)

(A) It was four years ago, but I remember enjoying my first week with my current employer, although there was a lot to take in and it was a larger company than I had worked for before. Some meetings had been pre-arranged for me, but before the end of the week I realised there were other people it would be helpful for me to talk to, and this was quite easy to arrange. I took the attitude from the first day that it was better to ask questions straight away if I was unsure about anything, rather than just guess. I am very happy to learn from other people. Of course, I felt a bit of trepidation; you always want to make a good impression and this puts a bit of pressure on, but I generally enjoy new situations.

(Q) Tell me about an occasion when you have had to say 'no' at work.

('Can you adapt your communication skills to be assertive?' is the message behind this question.)

(A) Quite recently, I had to refuse to give editorial space to an advertising client in one of our magazines. The editorial they had provided was not of a very high standard and I don't like to encourage people into thinking that they can get free space. If they want advertising, then they have to pay for it, unless they provide really good-quality editorial material. My advertising manager was not particularly happy, but I spoke to the client myself and explained the situation and she did take the point. Our conversation ended on friendly and constructive terms.

---

brilliant tip

People often misunderstand assertiveness. Assertiveness means being able to be firm and clear and hold to a course of action without being aggressive and bullying, or being pushed around by everyone. It is a key skill for many work roles and a handy life skill to boot.

(Q) Describe something you have done that was new and different for your organisation.

(You are being asked just how creative you are.)

(A) I started a series of short training sessions, which were run by different members of my team so they could give some basic ideas of how they worked and what their priorities were to the rest of the team. These sessions took only half an hour and we selected less busy times to do this. It worked very well; all staff understood more about how colleagues worked and communication improved. It also gave some people who had never led a session on anything a chance to do a bit of presenting.

Ⓠ Tell me how you go about solving a problem. Give me an example of a problem you have solved.

(Your problem-solving ability is being checked out here. This is a very important one because, whatever work you do, and for whatever type of organisation, it is pretty much on the cards that problems will come up.)

Ⓐ First of all, I try to analyse the causes that have led to the problem arising. Having done this, I try to group them together, e.g. are they mainly with people, resources, lack of appropriate information, etc? At this stage, it is usually pretty clear where the root of the problem lies, and this makes it much easier to work on a solution that is likely to be successful. We recently had a lot of problems servicing all our customer call-out requests to a really satisfactory level. In an effort to provide excellent service, we had moved to booking really precise time slots; in retrospect, we had probably made these too short. We worked with our service team, our booking staff and our customers to come up with something more flexible. It did involve looking at the problem from two very different perspectives.

Ⓠ Describe a special contribution that you have made to your employer.

(This question is designed to find out about your contribution to a team.)

Ⓐ For the past two years, I have coordinated our work-experience programme. This is a programme in which undergraduates join us for four weeks during the summer vacation to have some structured work experience in several of our departments. Most people are really happy to help out with this, but it is often hard to find a volunteer to run the whole thing, because it takes a lot of time on top of your normal workload. I think it is a really valuable way to build links between students and us and, although it sometimes drives me mad, I know my work is really appreciated by the firm and by the students.

Ⓠ Describe a situation where you believe your colleagues/company/department really rely on you.

(Your teamwork skills are being assessed here.)

Ⓐ I am often called upon if there is a confrontation with a client. I have a reputation for being calm and for being honest with people, and if there has been a situation where we are at fault I do follow it up and try to put things right. If the customer is being unreasonable, then I can usually talk them round without the situation becoming more heated.

> ### ✳ brilliant tip
>
> As you read through the questions in this chapter, you may disagree with some of the competences mentioned after each question, perhaps thinking that the question could equally well be there to assess another ability. Trust yourself, you are quite right; there is a great deal of crossover between communication, teamwork and relationship-building, and between problem-solving, creativity and innovation. Don't spend time in the real interview worrying about which competence is being assessed. The questioner may make this clear. If not, then your answers, if you have planned your examples carefully, should draw in the right material. It is just as hard to get an answer that adheres strictly to just one competence as it is to do this with a question.

Q **Describe the level of stress in your current job and what you do to manage it.**

(Your ability to self-manage is under scrutiny here.)

A I am working with quite a high level of stress at present, simply because regulations have come into force recently that affect my industry. I have had to oversee a large number of risk assessments and other new procedures in a very short time and I have to be able to demonstrate that these are in place to external assessors. In terms of managing the stress, I at least had the advantage that I knew these changes were coming, so I had a basic plan in place. I involved colleagues at an early stage and I took the decision to do one task at a time thoroughly, rather than scurrying round trying to do a little bit of everything at once. I certainly feel very busy, but I am in control.

brilliant tip

You can make a great impression with the combination of examples you choose to illustrate your competency. It does not matter whether they are from your school or university background or from employment, or really what the work situation was. What is always more important is how you coped with it, what your input was to doing something good, what steps you took to make a bad situation better, etc. Don't forget, though, your recent past is better than your ancient history.

Q **What do you think is the difference between a manager and a leader? Tell me about an occasion when you have applied your management and leadership skills.**

A I think that, in my current role, I have had to be both to some extent. I suppose I see managing more as organising work and controlling resources, whereas to me leadership is more about coming up with ideas and above all being able to take people with you, whether that is motivating staff to tackle something new or keeping morale and commitment going through troubled times. I think it is important to be able to see things through, as well as having innovative ideas. We had a merger of two departments recently, and I had to manage the amalgamation of two different administration systems. I think my leadership came in when I had to ensure that new members of staff felt involved and valued in the combined department.

Ⓠ Outline a situation where you had to make a decision that required careful thought. How did you go about this?

(Your thinking and decision-making skills are being tested here.)

Ⓐ Fairly recently, we had to decide whether to outsource all our public relations work to a consultancy. We had been doing it in-house for many years. Although I was not the only one involved in the discussions, my role as head of marketing meant that in the end the final decision came down to me. My decision was based on talking to colleagues, on exploring financial implications and on discussions with consultants who might take on the work. In the end, we decided to continue as we were; part of this decision was based on intuition as well as research.

(Clearly, this is an answer from someone senior and established in his or her career. At an earlier stage in your career, a quite different type of decision could provide an answer, as follows.)

Ⓐ One difficult decision I had to take was whether to try to defer a job offer that I had received just before I graduated, so that I could go travelling for six months. It felt risky to me: if the employer said 'no', I could cope with the disappointment of not travelling but I was worried that they might think I lacked commitment or would become restless. I instinctively felt that I could be open with the senior person who had interviewed me, but it still worried me. I talked to friends, my personal tutor and my careers adviser. In the end, I decided that honesty was the best policy and that I could genuinely reassure the company that

I would not harbour any negative feelings if they refused. As it turned out, they did want me to start work straight away and that turned out to be fine.

(Q) Describe a stressful situation that you have had to deal with.

(A) Quite recently, a group of overseas visitors was booked for a tour of my department, but the international office had forgotten to let anyone in the department know. I was in the middle of dealing with an enquiry when the group turned up expecting a tour and plenty of useful information. I did feel stressed because I was unprepared and I was annoyed at other people's inefficiency. I had to think on my feet, get someone else to take over what I was doing and give my tour and presentation. Actually, it went really well; the adrenalin probably helped. People asked a lot of questions and I was on quite a high at the end of it.

Nightmare to avoid

Don't use the interview to test your interviewer's stress-management capacity. On one occasion, an interviewee's bag started to make a strange cooing noise that sounded unlike even the most up-to-the-minute mobile-phone tone. The interviewers ignored it until the bag started to fidget and rustle, but the interviewee acted as if nothing was happening. It finally emerged that the candidate had decided to rescue an injured pigeon on her way in and, having no time to do anything else, had simply stuffed it into her bag. Unfortunately, one of the panel members had a bird phobia.

(Q) Tell me about a time when you changed your priorities to meet the expectations of others.

(They want to know if you can be flexible.)

(A) It is always difficult providing all the staff training you would like, within the time and financial constraints, and as we were just about to go through some restructuring I was very keen that we should have a team-building course of some sort for everyone involved. There was so much uncertainty around that many colleagues wanted a session on managing change. I was concerned that this might end up being a rather vague session that might not achieve much. I decided that, as feelings were so strong, I would have to put what would have been my priority choice to one side on this occasion. Actually, in the end, we got a very good trainer and the course on change led to some really constructive work on team roles.

Q Tell me about an occasion when you have used a creative approach to solving a problem or improving a situation.

(They want to know whether you are a creative thinker.)

A I took a job in customer services soon after graduating. Most of the work was dealing with telephone enquiries. Because we had so many different types of customer from different types of company, selling different products, etc., we were all dealing with every kind of enquiry and I don't think I was the only one who found it difficult. I suggested to my line manager that we might divide into work groups dealing with specific types of enquiry, so that we could give a more thorough service. I thought I might be speaking out of turn because I was fairly new, but I tried to be diplomatic and enthusiastic and actually they did take it on board.

brilliant tip

You won't make a great impression by indulging in clichés. Keep your responses free of 'blue-sky thinking', working 'outside the box' or being like a teabag 'strongest when you're in hot water'. To use another cliché, this sort of thing cuts no ice with most interviewers. Clear, lively examples work to much greater effect.

Ⓠ Describe an improvement you personally initiated.

(They want to know whether you are a good problem-solver.)

Ⓐ When I was senior laboratory technician at the school of medical sciences, I organised a system to improve the amount of time for which expensive pieces of equipment were in use. I instigated a more formal booking system. Some lecturers and research students were worried at first that they would lose out but actually, after a short settling-in period, equipment was in use for 30 per cent more of the time and everyone agreed that the system was a great success.

Ⓠ Describe a work situation where you have had to deal with something on your own.

Ⓐ Quite recently, I had arranged with another colleague to put on a training event for staff from other sections. We had put some of the material together and the session was booked. Unfortunately my colleague had to go overseas at short notice, so I had to run the session on my own and do quite a lot of the final planning. I enjoy working with groups, but I found I needed to do some last-minute thinking about how to vary my style, so they didn't get bored of just one presenter. It went really well on the day.

Ⓠ What is the most exciting team project you have been involved with?

Ⓐ Last year I was part of a team developing some healthcare drop-in centres. What made it really enjoyable was working with people from many different professional backgrounds – getting new perspectives that you might not have thought of on your own was really valuable. I had particular responsibility for liaising with local communities and feeding this back to the group.

Ⓠ Do you prefer to work on your own or as part of a team?

(On most occasions, it is your teamwork ability that is being checked out here. Dysfunctional teams can cause real problems for employers.)

Ⓐ I really prefer working as part of a team, where everyone's input can make a contribution to a project or a decision. I have enjoyed working in project groups ever since my university course. If I do have to work on my own, however, I am quite willing to do so; I don't need constant advice and reassurance from others about what I am doing.

(As with any question, you need to consider the job you are applying for before coming up with an answer. The answer above is ideal if you know that teamwork is one of the selection criteria and you are aware that working with other people is an integral part of the work. If you are applying for something where you will have to work on your own for long periods, then you would frame this answer the other way round, emphasising that you are quite comfortable and self-sufficient working on your own. Then follow up with a comment about enjoying working with other people when the opportunity arises.)

Ⓠ Describe an occasion where you have failed to reach a goal you had set yourself.

(Self-management is being assessed here.)

Ⓐ When I left university, I decided to do a master's course part-time at the same time as I started my first job. When it came to it, I found there was a great deal to learn with my first company and the training was intensive. In the end, I had to drop out of the master's programme for a year or two. In a way, it did not matter, because I did not need it for my work, but at first I did feel disappointed. Having done the course a bit later, it has probably been easier anyway, as I have had far more real experience to back up what I have studied.

Q Describe a situation when you had to influence different groups of people with different perspectives.

A In one previous job, I was involved in organising a community arts festival – our town had not had one before. At public meetings about the proposed event, there were people who were really keen – local traders and voluntary arts groups, for example. There were also many local residents who were convinced that it would bring a lot of noise and mess and too much traffic into the area. There were also people who generally were on board but were worried about the financial implications. It was challenging dealing with all these concerns at the one meeting. My main tactic was to anticipate what most of the concerns would be before the meeting, so that I had a lot of factual information about similar events in other places. I also made sure that I listened to everyone's concerns and answered them as honestly as I could, so that people at least felt that their views had had an airing. In the end, the festival went off very well and it has become a biennial event. I notice that with this post there is quite a lot of liaison work with different stakeholder groups, so I may well be able to put some of this experience to good use here.

brilliant tip

One potential drawback with competence-based questions is that they focus on the past and don't ask 'What would you contribute?' To combat this, grab opportunities wherever you can. The answer to the preceding question and the first model answer at the beginning of this chapter are examples of this. Adopting this tactic is high-risk because you are going outside the strict remit of the question, but for interviewers trying to select from candidates who all give similar responses, it can pay dividends.

Ⓠ **Have you ever had to work with a manager you simply couldn't get on with? If you have, why and how did you deal with it?**

(They want to know whether you have good relationship-building skills.)

Ⓐ There's been only one manager that I found it really hard to get on with. His predecessor had been great to work with and for. I had a lot of autonomy, and I felt I could make suggestions and take direction if necessary. Above all, I felt very trusted and it was really motivating. I believe I was doing a good job too. Her replacement wanted to control everything, literally down to how many paper clips we could order for the department, and minor issues were in danger of turning into confrontations. My strategy was to make sure I did discuss every major issue with him when it came up and hope that my open approach gradually would be rewarded. It was an uphill struggle and I was glad when he left, but the situation undoubtedly improved between us. Other than that, I have always had excellent working relationships with my managers.

Ⓠ **Tell me about a situation where you have found yourself in conflict with a colleague.**

Ⓐ I disagreed strongly with a colleague about whether we should use an external consultant or take on a new marketing initiative ourselves. We both felt strongly and we were on the same level. On that occasion, his argument won the day, but we turned out to be very disappointed with the consultant.

Ⓠ **Describe a situation where you have had to negotiate for something you felt was important.**

Ⓐ During a time of financial cutbacks, we were no longer able to recruit staff automatically to replace posts if employees left. It meant that every departmental manager had to make an individual case to senior staff to fill posts. You had to begin with a written submission and follow this up with a discussion where you had to make a very good case for why you should be allowed to recruit. I certainly felt really motivated to negotiate as hard as I could and, on the whole, over the 18 months that this policy was in place, I had quite a high success rate.

Nightmare to avoid

One interviewer was trying to ascertain just what skills of negotiation and persuasion a particular candidate possessed. The candidate made a wholehearted and pushy attempt to sell the interviewer life insurance and a pensions plan. After the interview, it transpired that he had been trying to do the same to other candidates and staff around the office. Yes, demonstrating a skill in action may be useful, but mostly it is likely to backfire. This particular candidate was not applying for a position to sell any financial products and he was not recruited for the position. This kind of reality demonstration of your talents is best avoided.

Ⓠ **Tell me about an occasion where you had to take on the role of leader.**

(Leadership is the competence being checked out here.)

Ⓐ At university we did one joint project – there were six of us in the group – in which we had to produce a report based on interviews we held with middle managers working in ICT in many different employment sectors, including health, education, leisure, law and local government. As leader, I had to make sure that everyone was allocated a reasonable number of interviews, and I had to follow up to make sure that these were being done. We worked as a group to generate ideas to start with, but it was really down to me to make sure everything came together. I found a big part of my role was in encouraging people to feel confident about approaching organisations to find potential interviewees.

Ⓠ When you go on holiday, what kind of plans do you make, or do you prefer to be spontaneous?

(They want to know something about your planning skills.)

Ⓐ I usually mix some spontaneity with a fair degree of planning. I am quite prepared to book something at fairly short notice and be flexible about where I go, but after this I do start to plan in a bit more detail. I like to do research about where I am going, find out places of interest, what the transport system is like, etc. This way, I can book for attractions or events that I know are going to be popular and ensure I don't miss out. There's so much you can do ahead on the Web now, though I am still prepared to use a book. I don't like to plan every last detail though; it's good to have some space just to follow your mood.

brilliant tip

This last is a great example of a tricky question, including as it does, two options – your planning skills and your spontaneity. It is likely that your average employer sets more store by your planning skills than by exuberant outbursts of spontaneity. If you are spontaneous about holidays, be truthful about this, but add that you adopt a rather different approach at work.

Ⓠ Tell me about something you have learned and applied recently.

(They want to know how you acquire and apply knowledge and expertise.)

Ⓐ Certainly, over the past two years I have learned more and more about the value of praise and encouragement to people who work for me. I suppose I have always known this at an intuitive level, but a course I attended on staff motivation really spelled this out and I have made more of a conscious effort to include this in my dealings with people. As well as staff seeming to appreciate it and being more motivated, it does make it much easier to criticise or question where this is necessary or appropriate. People are much more willing to take this on if they don't feel got at and they do feel valued.

(This is a good answer for someone with experience and responsibility. Earlier in your career, you might have quite a different answer. Whatever example you use, try to make it something that has lasting effects and where you can explain how it has helped you, rather than something factual, such as having learned about a software system or an accountancy package.)

Ⓐ A few months into my first job and about six months ago, I attended a customer-care course. I was a bit negative about it because I was busy and I thought it was going to be full of obvious clichés. In fact, doing a lot of role-play exercises was really helpful, challenging and tremendously entertaining at times. There are aspects of that course – trying to solve a problem where possible by talking to someone more senior than myself and then getting back to the customer rather than just passing on the customer straight away – that have been really useful. This has increased my confidence, I have a better rapport with customers and I know my manager is happy with the change.

Ⓠ **Tell me about a time when you came up with a new idea to solve a long-term problem.**

(Including the word 'new' means they want to know whether you are an innovator.)

Ⓐ We went through a phase where we often found ourselves recruiting graduates into administrative jobs that did not specifically require graduates, but where graduates often applied, they did very well at interviews and usually were very good at the work. As well as basic administration, they were involved in some information research and were often required to answer questions from clients and from members of the public. The only drawback was that there was no real career path, and often these graduates would leave just as we were finding they were really successful from our point of view. I suggested that, although we had a team of only six people in the information section, there was no reason why there could not be two posts for senior information assistants. This meant there was one step up the career ladder that people could take, and it also gave them some supervisory and management experience. It definitely improved our graduate-retention rate.

(You might get the following response.)

Q So why didn't you just stop recruiting graduates?

A As I mentioned, they were usually really good at the job, though we also had some really excellent information assistants who were not graduates. We did not want to limit our options in that way – getting good staff, whatever their qualifications, was very important to us.

Q Tell me about a situation where you have had to be tactful.

(This is one of the many aspects of communication skills that are often checked.)

A When I was working for one mid-range fashion store, a customer returned a skirt because she said she had noticed a slight stain near the hem that she had not seen when she bought it. The mark was very small and I was also pretty certain that she had worn the skirt and then possibly spilt something on it. It was possible, however, that she was telling the truth, so on that occasion I decided to give her the benefit of the doubt. We were really busy, but it was not that I could not make time to deal with it; I did not want potential new customers to get a bad impression of the place. Besides, it would have been completely undiplomatic to say I simply didn't believe her.

Ⓠ Give me an example of your persistence.

Ⓐ At one of the recruitment organisations I worked for, we had quite long waiting lists of people who wanted to book interviews with us. I was concerned that sometimes we were losing potential clients because they had to wait. I suggested that we start up a system of really quick drop-in interviews, particularly first thing in the morning, at lunchtime and at the end of the day, so that people could pop in for a five- to ten-minute chat and then book something more in-depth. Colleagues were really worried about this at first; they thought that it would end up creating more problems than it solved and that they would feel rushed and stressed. We shared out these drop-in sessions and it did work out really well. Clients could at least go away with something to think about or work on, even if they had to wait. I really had to work hard to get people to give it a try; it took several meetings, a lot of encouragement and a preparedness to do the first session myself.

Ⓠ What would your colleagues say about your attention to detail?

(Your self-management is being checked here.)

Ⓐ I believe that they would say it was one of my strong points and something that one or two of them find quite irritating at times. When I have done any of those management-style questionnaires, I always come out with 'completer/finisher' as fairly near the top, although 'shaper' and 'ideas person' are high up as well. When I was a student, I did various data-input and statistics-gathering work and you had to be very careful to get things right. I think the impression that job made has affected my approach to what some people might see as dull routine.

Many organisations that use this method of selection will also incorporate this focus on competences into the way they check references. The forms they send out to your referees often list the competences that are important for the job you have applied for, so that the referee can rate you against each of these. If you are on good terms with your referee – and presumably you are not going to ask anyone who does not like you to give you a reference – then it is worth spending a little time with them discussing the abilities they are being asked to assess. Sometimes they have only to tick boxes, and this limits scope for comments, but sometimes they will be asked to give examples.

Don't be intimidated by this interviewing style. It is designed to be very fair and, as a candidate, it may also be easier to anticipate the kinds of question you are going to be asked.

Summary and reminders

Ensure your competence shines through.

1 Make yourself familiar with plenty of examples from your recent past that can demonstrate your competences.

2 Remind yourself what the competences for this particular job are; even if you don't have a list of them, you should be able to work them out for yourself.

3 Keep your examples personal and relevant.

4 Try to make some links to the job you are applying for as well as outlining the things you have already done.

5 Don't ramble on. These interviews in particular try to pack a lot in, so you don't get time to waste.

CHAPTER 9

Your Achilles' heel

Dealing with difficulties; your weak spots and their perceptions

This chapter shows you how to handle any weak spots and tricky issues in your career history, awkward questions, embarrassing pauses and mean interviewers. Unless you are one of those rare people so annoying to the rest of us, who have led a charmed life and found that every decision has turned out well and that fortune has always smiled on them, you are likely to have aspects of your past (be it poor examination results, a period of unemployment, a patchy work history, poor health record, etc.) that you don't want to be asked about at job interviews. Yet you know that, because these issues are part of your history, they are likely to emerge from your CV, application form or employment and character references, so they are likely to arouse a future employer's curiosity. Interviewers do want an explanation of results or circumstances that appear to contradict other evidence of your history and character, and leave them wondering 'Why?'

brilliant tip

Remind yourself that you have been called for an interview. You aren't there just to make up the numbers, so whatever drawbacks you think you have, they must like what they have seen on paper.

Before preparing answers to any tricky questions that may be applicable to you, you should remember that interviewers ask these things because they genuinely want to know. They want to ascertain whether some weak spot was a temporary glitch or reflects a more pervasive problem. There is a possible second reason why you may be questioned on these 'Achilles' heels' – interviewers know that you are likely to feel vulnerable on these and they want to see whether you become hostile or defensive, or whether you take the opportunity to use your skills of communication, persuasion, analysis and calm reason to offer plausible and convincing explanations.

A brief word about truth

This book does not promise to offer a rigorous analysis of the philosophical and moral place of truth in the competitive jungle of job hunting. It does, however offer some common-sense advice on this subject. If you are hiding something on your CV and/or during a job interview, you are unlikely to communicate so effectively or to be as relaxed and natural as you would like. Things that you have chosen not to say, fictional exam results, jobs that you invent or references written by your mum to enhance your case may well trip you up. Employers almost always take up references before they employ you and if you have to hide the truth at an interview, then you have to ask yourself how you are going to keep this up if you are the successful candidate. Remember, also, that if an employer finds out later that you have not been straight with them, they may use this as grounds for dismissal or other disciplinary procedures.

This chapter covers many of the issues about which candidates feel anxious – and some suggested ways to deal with these.

---

brilliant example

Get started by considering this sample question and model answer. This question and answer are followed by a quick analysis of what makes that answer a success.

Ⓠ Do you have any qualifications?

If you do, then this question won't make you feel vulnerable; if you don't, then you want to put together a good, open, enthusiastic response.

Ⓐ My main strength is in practical and relevant work experience. I have worked in the hotel sector for seven years and I have taken advantage of a lot of in-house training courses. I started as a receptionist as soon as I left school: I was impatient to be at work and earning a salary. In my current job as assistant manager, I have had experience of dealing with all kinds of issues, on the customer side and the human resources side. I would certainly be happy to take a relevant qualification if the opportunity arose; I think it could help me in the future and it is always useful to take an opportunity to step back and look at what you are doing. I don't feel that having no qualifications on paper has held me back so far.

Why this answer works:

- It does not avoid the fact that you have no formal qualifications, but it does avoid coming out with a surly and forbidding 'No'.
- It moves on quickly to demonstrate a commitment to training.
- It emphasises progress up the career ladder.
- It does acknowledge a bit of impatience and the possibility of an unwise decision in the past.
- It reassures that this decision has not had dire consequences.
- It expresses a positive attitude to education and learning in the future.

Try analysing some of the answers that follow in this chapter to see why they work. You can use the same technique when you are devising your own model answers.

Ⓠ I see that you got very good GCSE results and yet your A-level results are poor. What happened?

Ⓐ I was unsure of whether I wanted to stay on at school and do A levels; it was something my parents pushed for, but my heart was not really in it. I had become too interested in other things and I just didn't put in the effort I should.

(A possible follow-up question to this that could easily provoke a defensive response might be as follows.)

Q Can I take it, then, that if you don't like something, you stop working hard at it? What if we give you a job and you find there are parts of it you don't enjoy?

A I have had a good work record for the past three years since I left school and I have had no difficulty in handling routine and repetitive tasks during that time. I have grown up a lot since I was 17 and I seem to learn better at work, rather than in a school environment. I am doing an evening course in website design though, and I am really enjoying that.

Q There appears to be an eight-month gap on your CV. What were you doing during this time?

A I had been temping for the previous two years and I really wanted something with more of a sense of direction. With hindsight, I might have done better to wait until I had something permanent before I gave up the temporary work, but I really wanted to concentrate on my job search and concentrate on it 100 per cent. I wasn't expecting the job market to plummet so badly during that time. I got my act together by doing a short, intensive course in secretarial skills and was very pleased to get back into the work environment.

Q You only got a third-class degree. We are really looking for someone with a good honours degree. Why should we consider you?

(Remember, whatever they say, they have still chosen to interview you.)

A Of course, I was disappointed – I had hoped for an upper second and my first two years' results indicated that I would achieve this. I had a lot of personal problems during my final year which are well behind me and sorted out now, but they did affect my result. My individual and group project results were good and I think these developed the communication, time management and information-gathering skills that I need for this particular post – so I know I am strong on useful, relevant work skills.

Q From your CV, it looks as if you have taken six years out of the job market. How do you think you will fit in coping with the routine and the demands of work?

(Candidates should not have to see this as a negative area in their past, but sometimes it can feel that way.)

A Yes, I took a break from paid work to have my children and see them settled into school. I have not had salaried employment for the past few years, but I have actually been working very hard. Bringing up a family has ensured I can deal with the unexpected as well as the routine and I often work a much longer day than I did when I was in paid employment. Besides, I certainly haven't forgotten all the skills I used in the drawing office. I keep up to date with the relevant trade press and, more significantly, by doing some drawing work for friends.

brilliant tip

Choose positive words such as 'useful', 'considerable', 'extensive' and 'relevant'.

Avoid negative words and phrases such as 'only', 'a little', 'limited' or 'not much' when describing activities and experience.

Q You seem to have done a wide range of jobs that don't meet up to your qualifications: they are not 'graduate' jobs.

Ⓐ Getting some kind of work was more important to me than anything else. Actually I learned a lot about myself, how much I enjoy imparting information to people. I also discovered some gaps in my knowledge and experience, especially about working under pressure; there is not one job I have done that has not taught me something, even if it is only never to do that kind of work again.

Ⓠ **I see that you were made redundant by your last employer nine months ago. How have you coped with this?**

Ⓐ It was not a complete surprise because the company had been in financial difficulties for a while and many of us were aware that our jobs might be under threat. Nevertheless, it was a shock and very hard at first. I've always been someone with an optimistic attitude, but this field is competitive. I enrolled on an IT course to give me some new design skills very soon after I lost my last job and I have also been doing some voluntary work for my local secondary school, helping with computer skills classes. My CAD skills have certainly developed significantly since leaving my last company and I am very eager to get back into full-time work.

Ⓠ **You don't think you will have lost a bit of your edge and slipped out of the work routine during that time?**

(This is one possible, rather mean, follow-up question.)

Ⓐ Quite the opposite. I have filled my time constructively and increased my skills, but I really enjoyed work. I think my energy levels and enthusiasm are on top form and I intend for them to stay that way.

Ⓠ **I notice that you were made redundant after only eight months in a previous post: why do you think this happened?**

Ⓐ It was basically a last-in-first-out policy and the company folded completely six months after I left. It was a pity; they had had some good ideas and our design team worked well together. It was the smallest company I had worked for and I gained a lot from having to be very flexible.

Ⓠ **It looks from your CV as if you haven't had much work experience at all – other candidates we are seeing today are likely to have had far more.**

Ⓐ I did think about working for a year before I went to university and I had intended to take on a part-time job while I was studying. In fact, my father was very ill for a major part of my course and I ended up helping out a lot at home and spending time with him and my family. My course was quite practical and, as you can see, I got a good result even with all the stress going on outside. I really believe I am capable of doing this job and doing it well, and you do emphasise your high standard of training and induction.

Ⓐ It was really difficult to find the sort of work I wanted when I first left school. I was desperate to get into something with the media and it was hard for me to accept that that just might not be possible at that time. I did do some voluntary work for my local hospital radio and some unpaid work experience with two local newspapers – I guess I should have mentioned those on my CV.

brilliant tip

Emphasise all your valuable experience to make the best impression. It is common for job applicants to dismiss useful experience as irrelevant. Voluntary work, work-shadowing, work experience and helping out with a family business are common examples of topics that candidates neglect.

Q Why did you drop out of university before you had completed your course?

A It was the wrong subject and the wrong time and place for me. I had been reluctant to carry on with my studies and I am afraid my first-year results showed that. The evening job I was doing at the local sports centre was far more exciting to me and the manager was very happy with me. If I go back to studying I want it to be part-time and I want it to be a more practical course than the degree I started.

It is difficult when, as a candidate, you know that there are extremely private and personal reasons that have affected an area of your life at a particular time – it may have been a bereavement, serious illness of someone close to you, a broken relationship or marriage, or problems within your family at an important time during your schooling. You are reluctant to reveal information that feels personal and private, which might make you feel upset and your interviewer embarrassed and which quite frankly is beyond the scope of what a prospective employer has a reasonable right to know.

Balanced against this is your knowledge that the facts of your personal circumstances at the time offer a legitimate and understandable explanation for a drop in your work or academic performance. It is perfectly reasonable to say that you were affected by difficult personal circumstances that you would rather not discuss at an interview but, if it is something you feel comfortable about mentioning, then do so. A family break-up during your school examinations or a marriage falling apart just as you applied for a promotion might be something you would rather reveal and get out of the way. Even the least well-trained of interviewers should not then follow this up with a run of personal and intrusive questions. It is also helpful to add a comment suggesting that whatever a problem was it is now behind you and is not affecting your performance any longer. That, after all, is what the person who is contemplating paying your salary and investing in your training and development really wants to know.

Q **You have changed jobs frequently in the last few years. Does this mean you get restless if you are in any job for a considerable length of time?**

A Some of my recent moves have been because I have needed to relocate to different places for personal reasons. I am now settled here and have bought a property. Of all the jobs I have done in the past three years, I really enjoyed my work at the finance company. I have very good references from them and the work I was doing looks very similar to the responsibilities you list in your advert and job spec.

A Many of those jobs were temporary anyway and my employers in those situations were not expecting me to stay long, for example when I was providing Christmas or holiday cover. I did not want to commit myself to a career until I was more sure of the direction in which I wanted to go. My temporary job in the local planning department gave me my first real involvement with work that touched on environmental issues, and I have done a great deal of voluntary work with urban and rural environmental improvement projects, so I hope that demonstrates my enthusiasm and commitment to a career with your organisation – it feels like the opportunity I have been waiting for.

A In an ideal situation I would not have chosen to change jobs so often, but at the moment it has been easier to get short-term contracts than anything permanent. It has certainly meant I get up to speed in new situations very quickly, but I would prefer a more secure situation and the opportunity to gain more management experience.

brilliant tip

In the current economic climate many applicants will face the situation of frequent job changing, short contracts and periods of unemployment. Interviewers are not picking on you when they mention it; they need to know how you cope and what your strategies are when you are in a disheartening position.

Q How have you motivated yourself to keep looking for work since you were made redundant?

A I have tried to build a lot of structure into my job hunting and the most important thing I have done is to keep in touch with a regular network of contacts. This not only keeps my name out there, it also keeps me in touch with any new developments and ideas. That is how I heard that you may be looking for someone with my experience.

Q You have requested us not to approach your current employer for a reference. Why aren't you happy for us to do this?

A My current company may be looking at some cost-cutting measures and if they think I am looking elsewhere I may turn out to be one of them. I am quite happy with my work there, but I have been at that level for two and a half years now and I think the job you are offering is ideal. I feel sure I would enjoy it, but I can't guarantee that I shall be the successful candidate and I don't want to unsettle things with my current firm.

A My current manager has only been in the post for three months and if he were asked to write my reference I am not sure that he knows enough about my work, what it entails, what my strengths are, or to be able to do justice to my skills. I feel you would get far more relevant information from my previous boss, for whom I worked for four and a half years.

Q **Your reference shows that last year you had 15 days off work due to sickness. Is this a typical annual record for you?**

A No, far from it. Those 15 days were all in a block and it was because I had had an accident while on a skiing holiday. My attendance record up to then has been good.

Q **Apart from your annual leave entitlement and public holidays, how many days were you absent from work last year?**

A Four – two were for dental surgery and the other two for an extremely heavy cold that meant I was useless on the telephone, but I am usually pretty hardy.

(Health records are of concern to employers. Many organisations will use a pro forma reference request, which they send to your current employer or your nominated referee. This form usually contains a section asking for details of how many days you have taken off work due to sickness, so your interviewer may already have access to accurate information on this.)

Q **What is your time-keeping like?**

A Good, I am usually the first to arrive in the mornings and I dislike being late for a meeting, training session or anything. I think you owe it to your colleagues as well as your manager to be punctual.

Q **You left your last job without having another one lined up to go to. Wasn't that a bit risky?**

A Yes, I suppose it was, but I had never intended to stay in sales for that long and it felt like the right decision. There had been a lot of changes there recently and very few staff were happy. It takes a great deal for me to become discouraged. But I felt my wisest option was to leave and start looking for something else. The sales work was useful, especially dealing with people and working under pressure – two things that I have become very good at. I'm sure they would be valuable in your customer-support department.

Ⓠ One of your references suggests that you sometimes lose your cool in the office. What is your reaction to this?

Ⓐ It has happened very occasionally, but I have always been quick to apologise if I have been unreasonable and it has certainly never happened in front of a client. I am aware of it, so I make an effort to keep calm and explain what is annoying or frustrating me. I think most of my colleagues would say that, although I can be a little volatile, I am a helpful and supportive member of the department for the vast majority of the time.

Ⓠ Have you ever been asked to resign?

Ⓐ No, but I have come close enough to it to resign of my own accord rather than waiting to be asked. We had undergone a restructuring with a new manager, with whom I admit I did not hit it off, and yet I had worked successfully and productively there for ten years. I knew that cost-cutting and streamlining measures were on the cards and I just had to accept that I was not flavour of the month. It was hard, but it was a useful lesson and I spent an interesting 18 months working as an independent consultant.

Ⓐ No, I am pleased to say that is not an experience I have had to go through.

Ⓐ Yes. It was the first job I had after I left school. I really wanted to get into anything to do with cars and somehow I ended up working for an insurance company – I don't think it was ever going to work out.

brilliant tip

Don't shoot yourself in the foot. If you have had awful experiences, losing jobs through no fault of your own, or even as a result of your own actions – if this is in the past, and won't emerge through references – don't mention it.

What am I supposed to say?

Some interviewers will try to find out more about your strengths and weaknesses by confronting you with imaginary scenarios to see just how good you are at thinking on your feet. These questions are not designed with one 'right' answer in mind, so don't waste time agonising over the correct solution. What your interviewer is looking for is evidence of your common sense, your ability to take decisions under pressure and your capacity to know your own limits.

Q You are the manager of a large supermarket and you receive an anonymous telephone call saying that a number of the baby-food products you carry have been tampered with by a protest group. How do you react?

A I would suspect it was probably a hoax but, of course, I would take every precaution in case it were not. If I had an assistant, I would ask them to arrange to cordon off the baby-food aisle and see what could be done to stop any items getting through the checkouts. I would also make a calm announcement over the PA. I would telephone the police and also local press and radio to begin a recall of any suspect items. If I had no assistant, my priority would be to stop anyone buying any of the products in question and then contact the police.

Q You work for a company that has been involved in secret merger talks with another company. You are aware of this because it is your job to know, but you don't have any authority in these talks, or this deal. You are the last person in the office and you get a call from a member of the financial press saying that they have heard that this merger is taking place. What would you do?

A I would say that they would have to speak to one of the directors of the company and that unfortunately none of them was available at the moment. I would check the diaries and give them the earliest possible time when they could call back. If they pressed me, I would simply repeat my previous answer very calmly and very politely.

Q You run the research and development section for your company and you have one designer in your section who is brilliant at his job, but very difficult to work with, unpredictable, bad-tempered and unable to conform to the company rules on many occasions. Yet there is no doubt he helps you make a lot of money because on a good day his ideas are brilliant. How do you deal with this?

A I would have to look at whether we were losing other good staff because of him, how likely he would be to join one of our competitors if we got rid of him but, most importantly, whether there were things we could do to get him to work more effectively as a member of the whole team. I would start by talking to him and possibly involving the human resource department in this discussion, and together we would all agree clear targets for improvements with a specific review period. I might also offer training and support if this seemed appropriate.

brilliant tip

One potential difficulty with this type of question is that you won't have much time to answer. Ensure you get used to taking less time to think by getting a friend to confront you with scenarios that they dream up (friends are capable of being far meaner than many real live interviewers).

Interviewers should not ask you questions about sex, religion and politics. Indeed, many of these questions are illegal and you will find some advice on this in the following chapter. They can, however, ask you questions about current affairs and general knowledge. Unless you are facing a particularly devious interviewer, these questions are not designed to reveal your political leanings; they are designed to test your ability to express your opinion, formulate an argument, defend a point of view. They won't usually pick contentious issues.

Q What do you think of staging the Olympic Games in London?

A I think it's great. I think it will help the economy and, if tourism starts to decline as people become more concerned about air travel, the games might be just what we need to keep Britain buoyant. If everything is finished on time, it will be a good model of how we can meet challenging deadlines.

A I have real reservations about it, even though I am a sports enthusiast. I think it may be difficult to justify so much expenditure when there are so many other demands on public and private finance. Of course, I would not mind being proved wrong on this occasion.

Here are a few more current affairs questions to give you an opportunity to work out your own answers.

Ⓠ How would you improve the public transport system in this town/city?

Ⓠ What steps would you take to integrate the student population more effectively into the local community?

Ⓠ If you were suddenly given a million pounds to spend on improving this town, how would you spend it?

Ⓠ How would you encourage more young people to continue with their education?

Ⓠ Do you think people should be given incentives to recycle their rubbish, or be penalised if they don't?

Ⓠ Which story grabbed your attention in the news today?

Ⓠ What new law would you introduce?

Ⓠ What current law would you repeal?

Ⓠ How would you improve the state of the country's finances? (Well everyone is probably thinking about it).

brilliant tip

Think of questions of your own, especially any that relate to the type of work or the area of the economy in which you are seeking work.

Ⓠ If you were compiling a book of significant world events of the past decade, what events would you include?

Ⓐ I might try to shift the boundaries of your question a little bit and say what movements and trends of the past decade have been the most significant. In the longer term, I think these might have more influence than specific events. I suppose I would include the huge expansion in global communication, which seems to be changing so many businesses, and the speed with which information about anything can be got around the world. The expansion of Europe and the development of China's economy are likely to have long-lasting effects on world economic trends too. Of course, heightened awareness of security issues of all kinds is probably significant – the plans to introduce ID cards here in the UK, for example. On a personal note, I would like to think that an increasing awareness of environmental issues, especially energy consumption, will become a more significant part of everyone's thinking – at national and personal levels.

(It is OK to include personal comments in questions like this, but you do need to exercise caution. You would not make the same comments about global warming to an environmental pressure group as you would to an oil company.)

brilliant tip

If you want to make the right impression, it is especially important to be prepared for this type of question if you are going for a job in the media, policy development, lobbying, etc. You may also find you face this type of question related specifically to your own profession, e.g. education, health, the environment, the legal system, etc., so consider carefully the issues and talking points within your profession.

That was mean

There are some interviews where it is not so much the questions that hit a raw nerve with you, but problems about the interview itself: silences, questions you just can't answer or aggressive interviewers.

Silence may be golden – it may be a beautiful thing on a deserted beach under a starry sky – but it loses its poetry and magic when it causes an embarrassing void in the flow of an interview conversation. To make matters worse, not all interview silence is the same kind of silence. There is the silence that means you have not got a clue what to say; the silence that means you know what the interviewer is getting at, but it is an awkward question and you need time to think about it; or the silence where you believe you have given a thorough, cogent and complete answer and yet your interviewer lets you down – he or she does not respond with the next question. In all three instances, resist the temptation to tell a joke, sing a song or rush out of the room in tears; there are more effective ways to deal with the situation.

If you really don't know the answer to a question, then you should say so. This problem is most likely to occur if you are being asked technical/professional questions that you do not know the answers to at this stage, or if you are being asked to provide factual information of some kind.

A I am sorry, but that isn't an area I am familiar with at present, so I can't really give you any details on that.

A I am not familiar with that particular data management system, though I would imagine it is quite similar to others that I have used and I am usually quick to get to grips with new systems.

A I am sorry, but I haven't come across that particular term before. Would you mind clarifying it for me?

A I am afraid that is an area we did not cover on the course, but it is something I am very keen to learn more about.

A I'm afraid that isn't a situation I have ever had to deal with, but I believe I would deal with it in the following way.
(Then go on to give specific details.)

A That is a new area for me, so I am afraid I can't really answer that, but I enjoy acquiring new knowledge and I do learn quickly.

(A) That is not an area with which I am very familiar at the moment, but I see from your recruitment brochure that you offer a thorough induction programme and training opportunities, so I would like to take advantage of one of these if I were to be offered a position with you.

(A) I am not familiar with that legislation, but it is something I would make sure I brought myself up to speed on very quickly if you were to offer me this job.

(A) I have never used that software before, but I would be happy to do any necessary training either through your training department or on an external course if that was more appropriate.

brilliant tip

Make a good impression by being straightforward, by emphasising your ability to find out answers to what you don't know. Stay cool and confident – it counts for a lot.

Show some of your finer qualities in action, e.g., self-assurance, assertiveness, honesty and composure.

It is entirely acceptable to ask for clarification if you don't understand a question, though do this in a way that does not make your interviewer look silly. 'I've no idea what you're on about' is not a response that will endear you to your interviewer.

(A) I am sorry, I am not quite sure what you are asking. Could you ask me that question again, please?

(A) I am not sure where I should start with that. Please could you give me a little bit more of an explanation?

Asking for a few moments to think about your answer can immediately remove the anxiety factor from a silence.

Ⓐ That's an interesting question; may I have a moment or two to collect my thoughts?

Ⓐ There is quite a lot I could say about that; can you bear with me while I think about that for a minute?

(These responses are fine. Take it that you have overdone it if the interviewer goes away, makes a cup of coffee and deals with one or two telephone calls in the time you have taken to get your thoughts into order.)

If you are faced with a situation where you think you have given a complete answer, but a silence ensues because you are not asked another question, then you can always say:

Ⓐ Is there anything you would like me to add?

Ⓐ Should I go on to tell you a little about how my previous job gave me some useful experience of dealing with these types of problems?

Encountering an aggressive interviewer is an unpleasant but, happily, rare experience for a candidate. To some extent, this style of interview is out of fashion, and concerns about equal opportunities plus an increasing reliance on competence-based interviews make it unlikely to find favour. Nevertheless, your interviewer could be having an off day, be under a lot of pressure or simply not have the ideal personality for interviewing.

An employer may wish to determine how you react in a hostile situation and to discover aspects of your personality through other means than just asking you to describe them. Keeping calm and avoiding hitting your adversary is a fundamental starting point. It is, however, important that you don't crumble under the pressure and that you continue expressing your well-prepared answers clearly and assertively.

brilliant tip

Aggressive-sounding questions often begin with the word 'why'. 'Why did you take this decision?' 'Why did this problem arise?' Just stay calm; don't be panicked into giving a poor answer and try not to take the whole thing too personally.

Remember the questions are not any more difficult, even if they are being asked in an unpleasant way. It may be that the position you have applied for will mean that you are placed with some fairly aggressive colleagues or clients and if your interviewer is aware of this, they want to ascertain that you will be able to cope.

Once in a while, you are nice, your interviewer is pleasant, but circumstances are difficult. Your interview is constantly interrupted by telephone calls or by people bursting into the room. Your interviewer probably feels even more flustered than you by this (unless it is some bizarre psychological test). Bad planning, time pressure or staff shortages are more likely explanations. Take a note of where the conversation broke off, so that you can get it back on track quickly if your interviewer is struggling with 'And where were we?' One candidate being interviewed for a job at a company based in a coastal town had their interview interrupted because the interviewer was a member of the local lifeboat crew and he was summoned to a rescue – so some interruptions have to be forgiven.

Summary and reminders

You can deal with even the most awkward, challenging or disconcerting questions by careful thought and planning.

1 Prepare ahead for any areas where you know you may be vulnerable.

2 Ensure that those people whose names you are giving as referees know this beforehand and have given their permission for you to do so. This is not only courteous but it means, if there are any areas of concern, they may be prepared to discuss them with you in advance.

3 Accept that some interviews will go badly and you can't always redeem the situation.

4 Be candid and truthful, but don't give people information they don't ask for; you don't have to drag all the skeletons out of your cupboard.

5 Remember that you would never have been called for an interview if there was not a real chance that you could be the successful candidate, so be positive.

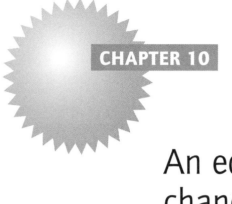

CHAPTER 10

An equal chance of success

Equal opportunities, positive thinking and the selection process

Everyone who is called for an interview must accept that he or she might not be the best candidate. Unless you are going for a promotion within a company where you know which colleagues are applying, or you are among a group of undergraduates all chasing the same company, the other candidates are an unknown quantity. What you do want to be assured of, however, is that you are being given a fair chance; that you haven't just been called to interview to make up the numbers and that the selection process will not discriminate against you on such grounds as age, gender, ethnic background, sexual orientation, health or disability.

Unfair discrimination

Unfair discrimination is treating someone less favourably than another on grounds such as race, gender or disability. Many groups of applicants who might be discriminated against have protection under the law.

Whatever preparation you have undergone, you cannot, as the one being interviewed, compensate either for the illegal actions or the poor attitude of interview panels. What you can do is prepare yourself to be as positive and constructive as possible, and also to at least be aware, if you find yourself being asked to answer what you regard as inappropriate or unacceptable questions. It is beyond the scope of this book to offer a comprehensive guide to the law, but there are separate pieces of legislation concerning discrimination on grounds of gender, race and disability. More recent legislation has made it illegal to discriminate on grounds of age, though the main thrust of this is to protect older people from losing their jobs. Other recent employment regulations give protection from discrimination on grounds of sexual orientation and religious belief.

brilliant tip

It is best to prepare for any interview assuming that you are not going to be discriminated against, so don't spend hours poring over relevant legislation.

Employers are, of course, quite reasonably entitled to reassure themselves that you are capable of doing the job. Aware and experienced interviewers will ask questions in an *appropriate* way.

brilliant example

Get started by considering this sample question and model answer. The question and answer are followed by a quick analysis of what makes that answer a success.

Ⓠ **What experience have you had of working with diverse groups of people?**

Ⓐ I have had plenty of opportunities and I have always enjoyed working with different people. On my course at university, there were students from 17 different countries in my year and our oldest student was 57. I found that learning from people who had different cultural perspectives and different life experiences was really valuable, and it made seminar discussions very interesting. It did open my eyes to cultural issues that I had never thought about, such as different ways of handling confrontation, disclosing personal information, etc. I have tried to keep that awareness going during my working life. I think it is essential that any company that wants to be successful in a global market has a really diverse staff group, and I would feel more uncomfortable if this were not the case.

Why this answer works:

- It is more than a general paying of lip service to equal opportunities policies.

- It is probably better to give an example like the one of the university course, rather than simply presenting a list of the groups that you feel might be discriminated against.

- It suggests you hold on to and build on to useful lessons you learn in life.

- It emphasises the benefits to the business concerned of cultural diversity.

Try analysing some of the answers that follow in this chapter to see why they work. You can use the same technique when you are devising your own model answers.

The question you have just considered is quite a kindly question, easing you into thinking about equal opportunities, and it is a question that is assessing your attitudes. Many of the questions that follow can be far more hostile and may say more about your potential employer than about you.

Q **With this job there are sometimes occasions when you have to work until 7.30 p.m. at short notice. Would you be able to do that?**

A I understood this from your job description and it would not be a problem at all.

(Rather than the following question, which should not be asked.)

Q I see you have children. What arrangements would you make for their care if you were required to work late?

(This second version makes you feel you have to outline your childcare arrangements and diverts from the main purpose of the interview – to sell yourself. Try using an answer similar to the one above.)

A I considered all these issues carefully before I applied for this job, so I would be quite prepared to undertake this late work when it was necessary.

(In other words, it's none of your business, so long as I can fulfil my work commitments, but I am too polite and sensible to say so.)

An example of an effective and poor way of questioning an interviewee for whom English is not their first language:

Q Tell me about your writing skills.

Q How good are your verbal communication skills?

Rather than:

Q I see from your CV that you arrived in the UK only two years ago and that English is not your first language. How would you cope?

A I had studied English at school, so my written English was reasonable before I arrived here. I have much preferred learning by using it, though, and I feel happy to hold a conversation on any subject. Actually, in one of my temporary administrative jobs I was complimented on my good command of the English language. I would be happy to learn other European languages too; it is something I enjoy and comes very easily to me.

> ### brilliant tip
>
> Remember you have a choice. You may believe that you have been asked an inappropriate or even illegal question in an interview, but common sense and your choice as an individual must dictate your reaction. You may still want the job and be favourably impressed with everything else you have found out about the organisation. In this case you may decide it is not appropriate to do anything other than answer the offending question as diplomatically and positively as you can. It is never easy to decide whether to be a trailblazer for the personal rights of yourself and other individuals or whether to follow the more pragmatic route.

Here are some examples of ways of dealing with nasty questions.

Q You don't mention your age on your CV – how old are you?

A I am in my early forties and I have had more than twenty years' work experience, the last five years in a human resource department, and I believe all the experience I have had is very useful for this post. I have had so many opportunities to develop my interpersonal skills, working with other colleagues, different work teams and members of the public.

A I am not sure why you need to know my age. I have had five years' experience since graduating and I passed my professional examinations two years ago. I can certainly give you more details of specifics of my last job.

Q You are older than most of the staff we employ here. How do you think you would fit in?

A I think fitting in is all about personality and about a real interest in the job and has little to do with age. I noticed that most of the staff in this agency, probably in most advertising agencies, are younger than me. I am comfortable working with any age group. I was the oldest student on my course, but I fitted in socially as well as academically – I have some creative ideas and, after all, I have been a consumer for longer than most of your staff and know what makes me buy something.

Q The manager here is a lot younger than you. How do you feel about being managed by a younger person?

A I am far more interested in their qualities as a manager than in their age. I have had managers of various ages in the past and I have never found it to be an issue. I think it can be highly beneficial to have a mix of ages and types of experience – it provides a good opportunity for learning.

Q We hadn't realised you were so young when we called you for interview. Do you think you could do the job?

A Of course; the job really appeals to me. I love sport and the idea of working at a leisure centre. I have had a lot of unpaid but really good experience, helping out with my family's retail business. I have often looked after the place on my own and I am very used to dealing with people.

Employers are not supposed to discriminate on grounds of age and, if you have been called to interview, you can assume that they are not discriminating. Many attitudes about being either too old or too young for a job are deeply ingrained in our work culture, so you may well find yourself having to answer this type of question.

Q Would you expect to go on working beyond the statutory retirement age?

A I would certainly consider it, especially if I am enjoying work as much as I am at present and remained fit and healthy. I enjoy sharing ideas with colleagues of different ages and I find it hard to imagine suddenly switching off.

There are some questions you should never feel obliged to answer, even though you want to stay on the right side of your interviewer, questions such as: 'Do you have a girlfriend/boyfriend?' 'Are you gay?' 'Who did you vote for at the last election?'

brilliant tip

If you are asked several unpleasant and unfair questions, you may want to ask yourself whether this is really the kind of employer you want to work for.

Q Are you married?

(A question that really should not be asked.)

A I am, but my working life and my home life are two separate things. I enjoy my current job very much, especially since I have taken on more management responsibility.

A No I am not but, married or not, my main current interest is in developing my career as an architect. I have followed your recent projects with great interest and, as you can see from my portfolio, my designs and aspirations seem to fit very well with what you are looking for.

A I don't really see the relevance of that question to this interview.

(You run the risk of sounding hostile with this final response, but that may be exactly how you feel and it may be the only response with which you feel comfortable.)

Q Do you have children?

(This is another naughty one.)

A No, I do not.

A Yes I do, two, who are both at school. Having this dual role has made me a very effective time manager and it goes without saying that I am quite able to keep my domestic life and my working life well separated.

A I am not sure of the relevance of that question to my application for this position – I don't really feel comfortable answering such personal questions.

Q **From your CV, I see that you arrived in this country only three years ago. How are you fitting into the job market here?**

A I am doing very similar work to that which I did before I came here – working on major construction projects – and I have been qualified as a quantity surveyor for five years now. I am enjoying work here and if you were to offer me a job I could be a great asset on some of your overseas projects later on.

Q **You have met staff in the office here. How well do you think you would fit in with us?**

A The staff I met seemed very friendly and very committed to family and community law. I would imagine that many of your clients in this locality are from different ethnic groups, so I would probably do your image a lot of good.

brilliant tip

You don't have to read up on equal opportunities legislation to prepare for an interview, but knowing the law is on your side may be useful if you do have particular concerns. You don't need to tell the employer you are an expert on recent legislation, but just knowing it will probably make you feel more in control.

There is now legislation in place covering discrimination on the grounds of age, gender, race, disability, religion, sexuality and sexual orientation. Each of these specifics is covered by a different piece of legislation and there is plenty of information on all of them on the Web. In all cases, the law applies to the recruitment and selection procedure as well as to what happens once you have the job.

Location, location, location

It is understandable that interviewers will want to know how you are placed if either your job or the organisation is likely to relocate or if there is a lot of travel involved.

Q We are exploring the option of relocating our headquarters to another city. Would you be able to relocate if we did?

A Yes I would. I am established here and I am buying a local property, but if the job was right for me I would definitely be prepared to consider relocating. What kind of assistance do you provide for your staff in terms of a relocation package?

Q If we offered you this job in our IT support department it would be necessary for you to provide some weekend cover and also to be on call for emergencies on a rota. Do you have any problems with that?

A That would be fine. In my current job I provide some weekend cover and I would be quite happy to continue this; I had anticipated it anyway. It would be useful to know how far in advance you plan your rotas, but I can usually be flexible.

Q How geographically mobile can you be?

A I realise that this post could involve transfers and I bore that in mind when I applied. I like this area, but for the right opportunity I would undoubtedly consider moving.

Q **There is a lot of travel involved with this job, and you would be away from home a lot. Do you have any problems with that?**

A None at all. I simply see it as part of the work. I know it is not always as glamorous as it sounds, but I am pretty adaptable, good at getting on with work when I am not at my desk. I had to do a fair bit of that in my previous job.

Q **We like staff to attend our social functions: how do you feel about this?**

A In principle I am quite happy about it. Of course it depends what the function is and what other commitments I have at the time, but it can be really good to get to know colleagues in contexts other than the day-to-day working environment.

(Employers cannot insist that you attend social functions, unless this is part of your job description and role, e.g. organising events).

Q **How long do you intend working for us?**

A I see this move as real career progress and if all goes well I would like to work here for the foreseeable future. I know that staff turnover can present real difficulties in social services and I feel it is important to stay put, to get to know the area, the clients and the department and the way it works. Ultimately, I would like to take on more management responsibility here.

Q **I've employed people doing a job-share before and I just seemed to have twice as much administration and a lot of headaches. How can you reassure me that it will be different this time?**

A I'm sorry that you've had such a poor experience. I have job-shared once before and it worked really well. I have met the person I would be sharing with here and we both have a real commitment to making it work for you. I am sure the most important thing is good communication between the two of us, and between us and everyone else here, especially our line manager. It would probably be really useful to make sure that there is half a day a week when we are both here at the same time, so that anything that needs to be discussed can be. With e-mail, though, even if this were not always possible, I would certainly ensure that I kept my partner really well-informed of any outstanding issues and anything that needed to be followed up. You do get two people's ideas and energy, even if you do have a bit more administration. I am sure it would work really well in this instance.

(Q) I see you have been working part-time for the past three years. This is a full-time post. Have your circumstances altered in some way that requires you to look for a permanent job?

(A) I was doing an evening course in interior design and, although it was only two evenings a week, I had to do quite a lot of private study as well. Now that I have finished that course, I am certainly able to take on full-time work.

(They could follow this with something like the next question.)

(Q) Do you find it difficult to manage your time, then, if you have demands coming from several directions?

(Don't get ruffled if they try to catch you out like this.)

(A) Not at all. I rather enjoy having more than one project on the go. I worked alongside my time at university and I was a course rep in my final and busiest year. I think you often find imaginative ways of dealing with problems by dealing with different issues in various areas of your life. The design course was very important to me: I had to save up to do it, and I wanted to do well. It has certainly encouraged me to be more creative and imaginative, and I already have some really good ideas that I am sure would work well if you offered me this position. I can give you one of my ideas if you like.

(Don't be offended if they don't want to follow up on an offer like this: time constraint is always a big problem for interviewers and interviewees.)

ⓠ Do you have any personal issues outside work that are likely to affect your ability to do this job?

(Although this is an unpleasant question, it is not actually an illegal one. Yes, if someone who had applied to be a steeplejack had a phobia about heights, then it might be reasonable for the employer to know about this, but usually highly personal information should not be relevant. You might be asked this sort of question if the emotional demands of the job are very high, e.g. if you are working in some aspects of mental health, social care or medicine. Some US companies seem to like asking this sort of forthright question. Resist the temptation to say 'None of your business', but don't be drawn into giving away personal information that should not concern your employer.)

ⓐ I have always found that I am very good at keeping my personal life and my work life separate. I have often found that if one area of your life is a bit problematic, then it is very useful to be able to concentrate on work, but at present everything is going steadily and wanting to make this career move is my focus. Although I say I keep work and other parts of my life separate, I have always been happy to socialise with work colleagues if it turns out to be that sort of a work team.

Able to do the job

Applicants with disabilities face particular concerns about the selection process. Even with the legal protection of the Disability Discrimination Act you can still find yourself in the position of having to reassure the interviewer in addition to the usual demands of an interview.

Q You mentioned on your CV that you have had a health problem. Could you tell me a little more about that?

(In October 2010 it became illegal to discriminate on health grounds, but not illegal to ask about it.)

A Yes, during my final year at university I developed ME and that is undoubtedly the reason why I got a third-class degree, rather than the upper second that had been predicted. All my course work up to that time had received very high marks. I am pleased to say that it has responded very well to treatment and I am now feeling a great deal better, much more energetic and ready to take on full-time employment.

Q You say on your application form that you are registered disabled and that you have a visual impairment. What implications would this have for us if we offered you a job?

A I am sure it wouldn't have any implications for you. I would require a computer with a reasonably large screen and some specialised software, but you may already know that there is external funding available for that, so it would not have any cost implications for you. As far as doing the job is concerned, I am working successfully in a similar environment, though the job you are offering looks even more closely related to my MSc than the work I am currently doing.

Q You mention that you are dyslexic. Are there any ways in which you think this affects your work?

A Well, I must admit that spell-checkers and other computer facilities are a marvellous invention as far as I am concerned, but as I work as a graphic artist my design skills and imagination are the key things. I think one of the reasons they are as good as they are is because I have always had to find other ways than straightforward words to put my ideas across.

Picking the moment

Deciding when to tell an employer something that you feel they should know, but that you feel might be negative, is always difficult and it is really a matter of personal preference. Some candidates like to get a possible problem out of the way quickly and then get on with trying to get the job. Others feel that revealing something will be easier if they already have a rapport with their interviewer.

brilliant tip

You should be the one to decide when and how to disclose information; then you can feel calm, relaxed and in control.

For candidates who have a criminal record, this can be a huge additional source of anxiety and the details are complicated. Basically, however, there are many offences that are deemed 'spent' after a certain period of time. If you have a spent conviction, you do not have to mention it.

Q Do you have a criminal record?

A No, I do not.

For any job that involves working with children or vulnerable adults you will be subject to a Criminal Records Bureau check and this check also covers 'spent' convictions. You may also be subject to vetting by the Independent Safeguarding Authority (ISA), though these procedures are under review at present.

> ## ✸ brilliant tip
>
> If you think you might encounter prejudice or cultural bias, pre-empt problems by considering what some of the assumptions in the minds of your interviewers might be. Then work at ways to put their minds at rest without being uncomfortable about who you are and being positive about what you have to offer.

Fighting misconceptions

There are, unfortunately, misconceptions held by some, not by all means all, employers. Even with equal opportunities legislation in place, you can't legislate against what people think. Discrimination can be subtle and it can be unintentional. Anticipating some of the misconceptions you might encounter can help you to have firm and appropriate responses. These misconceptions include:

- Women of child-bearing age may soon go off on maternity leave.
- Women (and single men) with children may take a lot of time off to cope with domestic emergencies.
- Women may suddenly relocate to follow their partner's career moves.
- People with disabilities may cost the company money in terms of adaptations, special equipment, etc.
- Someone with a disability might take a lot of time off sick.
- Applicants from other ethnic groups may have cultural values that differ from those in the organisation.
- We don't have a diverse mix of staff here at the moment, so applicants from other backgrounds might not feel comfortable here.

- Qualifications and experience gained in another country probably won't be as useful as qualifications and experience acquired in this country.
- Black people are very aggressive.
- Older people won't learn as quickly.
- Older people won't cope with having a younger manager.
- Young people are likely to be restless and want to move on.

Unreasonable, irrational and unfair as these assumptions are, you are better equipped to deal with them if you have considered them yourself. Obviously it is pointless to look for problems where they don't exist – if your prospective employer is showing no concerns (and in a perfect world this should be the case), don't raise concerns that they simply don't have.

Larger firms and organisations are likely to have a stated equal opportunities and diversity policy. This is not always the case among smaller outfits. This is not to imply that all large employers are good on equal opportunities while small ones are bad. It is easy to have a policy, but ensuring its implementation is a different question. A firm may have no stated policy and yet its ethos, attitude and commitment to equal opportunities may be laudable and genuine.

The way in which you are likely to experience the difference between the two, if you are called for an interview, is that larger organisations may be able to use trained interviewing staff, to have a standard set of questions that they ask all interviewees and to be in a position where they may be asked to justify their selection. Each candidate may be scored against specific selection criteria so that the interview panel can demonstrate that they have chosen the most suitable candidate.

brilliant tip

If commitment to equal opportunities is one of the criteria for a job for which you are being interviewed, you will be asked about it at the interview. Prepare an answer in plenty of time. It can be raised as an afterthought, by which time you are running out of steam.

Q Explain what you understand by an equal opportunities policy.

A My understanding is that every employee and everyone with whom we deal will be treated fairly, regardless of age, gender, sexual orientation, ethnic and cultural background, disability or social background.

(Questions and answers like these can lead to you feeling you have simply gone through every category you should on a checklist. A more meaningful approach that you could encounter would be the following.)

Q What steps would you take to help implement our equal opportunities policy if we offered you a job in this department?

A First of all, I would look at all the information we supply for our clients to answer two questions. First, is it accessible to everyone and, second, does it carry positive images to represent all the different client groups we have? If the answer to either of these questions was 'No', then I would look at ways of improving access, not just on disability issues but on things like leaflets in different languages and more information on our website. Those are just some initial thoughts.

To some extent, interviewers believe what you tell them. This does not mean you can just make up any old collection of spurious qualifications and imaginary periods of employment, but they won't normally argue that an experience is insignificant or irrelevant if you have described it as valuable. They won't challenge your assertion that you possess a certain quality, so long as you can offer evidence of an occasion when you used or developed it.

For this reason, the more positive you are about dealing with any doubts, stated overtly or hinted at during your interview, the better the impression that you will make. Being mature equals wisdom, common sense and breadth of experience. Being from a different background denotes different ways of looking at things, new ideas, the overcoming of obstacles and the opportunity to bring valuable diversity to a workforce. Train all your thoughts and your preparation in this direction and the boost this will give to your self-confidence is almost guaranteed to rub off on your interviewer.

Summary and reminders

Do what you can to ensure that you have an equal chance of getting any position for which you apply.

1 Find out as much as you can about your prospective employer's attitude to equal opportunities. Do they mention it in their advert – do they have a stated policy? What kind of images do you see on their website and in their other publicity?

2 Amass all your positive selling points exactly as you have done for any other aspect of the interview, but paying special attention to areas that you see as potentially sensitive.

3 Learn how to be assertive and ensure that you know how to distinguish this from being aggressive. Avoid being passive.

4 Be confident in articulating your selling points.

5 Be realistic – you may have given a weak interview, but try to assess where the fault really lies.

6 If you feel that you really have been treated unfairly and on discriminatory grounds, then seek professional advice.

CHAPTER 11

Turning the tables

Your questions answered –
what do you need to know?

'Is there anything you would like to ask me?' This question is often asked towards the end of an interview and it is another of those questions that candidates worry about. Supposing you haven't thought of anything, or what if all the questions you have so carefully prepared have been answered by the extensive and relevant information you have been given during your interview or through informal conversations with other employees before your interview?

If you really feel that everything that you want to know has been covered fully elsewhere, then say so, as politely as possible. Versions of some of the following may ease your anxiety:

Ⓐ Thank you, but I have been able to find so much out from your website – it has been a really useful way to find answers to all my questions. It is a very well-designed site and so easy to navigate.

Ⓐ Your graduate recruitment online information is really informative and it answers all the questions I have about the company and about your training scheme. I found the profiles of recent graduates really useful. I would like to know a bit more about what professional qualifications I could work towards.

Ⓐ I was able to find out so much from your colleagues when we had our tour of the production line and offices this morning that I don't think there is anything else I need to ask you at the moment, thank you.

There are no prizes for asking really obscure and difficult questions, least of all those questions that might make you look smarter than your interviewer – that doesn't go down well. If you have learned their annual turnover figures for the past decade or know the names of every member of staff in the post room, keep this to yourself and take note that, with such a brilliantly trained memory, you may have a great future in pub quiz teams.

brilliant tip

Use the opportunity to find out more about the organisation, its work and your potential role within it, and remember this really is a useful opportunity for you.

Don't feel you are only offered the chance to ask questions to see how clever you are.

Don't let thinking about this question divert your attention throughout the rest of the interview – worrying as your planned questions are answered one by one.

Preparing before the interview can help you to come up with some sensible questions which indicate that you are both intelligent in your approach to the job and have thought seriously about your possible future within that set-up, your training needs, your prospects and how the company might reward your efforts. The majority of the interview is dedicated to allowing the company to assess whether they think you have got what it takes. It is perfectly reasonable that you should want to know whether they have got what it takes to satisfy your choices, ambitions and goals.

Use the following questions to develop your own questions related to the specific job you are applying for.

Q **What are some of your current big projects?**

Ⓠ **What projects/campaigns/developments do you have planned that you are able to talk about?**

Ⓠ **Which projects would the successful candidate be working on initially?**

Ⓠ **How do you see your market holding up in the current economic situation?**

Ⓠ **To what extent am I likely to be working on my own?**

Ⓠ **To what extent am I likely to be working as part of a team and are staff involved in more than one project team at the same time?**

Ⓠ **To what extent would I have the opportunity to use and develop my language skills?**

(Clearly you can substitute any relevant skill here: Web design, supervisory, research, technical, entrepreneurial, etc. – whichever are pertinent for you and logically might be developed as part of your role within the organisation.)

Ⓠ **What kind of training will I have the opportunity to take if I am offered this job?**

(You should be able to make this mention of training more specific, e.g. management training, training on your computer system, customer-care training, or whatever is relevant to the position concerned.)

Ⓠ **Do you encourage staff to take relevant professional qualifications?**

Ⓠ **What support, if any, do you give to staff who take further professional qualifications?**

Ⓠ **What is your policy on staff development?**

Ⓠ **How much contact am I likely to have with other departments/external organisations/clients/customers?**

Q Are there particular management models that you favour?

Q In which of your offices is the position based initially?

Q How much autonomy can I expect to be given within my work?

Q How much of a requirement is there to be geographically mobile?

Q How soon would I be expected to relocate?

Q Are there likely to be any opportunities for overseas travel/travel within the UK?

Q What approximate starting salary do you have in mind?

Q Are salary reviews related to performance?

Q When might I expect my first salary review?

Q What salary progression might I reasonably expect over the first three years?

brilliant tip

You can create a good impression by making your questions about salary more wide-ranging than your immediate starting pay – linking the discussion to longer time-frames and sounding confident about your own performance can be a great strategy. It is also completely understandable and expected that you should want to know how much you will be paid.

Q Do you have a formal appraisal system?

Q How do you measure and monitor staff performance?

Q If everything goes well, where might I expect to be in two/three/five years' time?

Q How soon could I reasonably anticipate a promotion?

Q What are some typical career paths of graduates you have taken on in the last two years?

Nightmare to avoid

One candidate let slip during an interview that he had applied for a job with a particular employer because work made him rather tired and he thought it might be the sort of place where he could have a bit of a rest. Of course, he was not offered the post.

Q Approximately how many hours a week do you expect your staff employed at this level to work?

Q Do you have a policy on flexible working hours?

Q Do you have examples of staff who have been able to work flexible hours?

Q How effective has your equal opportunities policy been?

Q How do you feel about someone wanting to work on beyond statutory retirement age?

Q Do people here tend to socialise outside work?

brilliant tip

Make sure you know what organisational culture means – it is a combination of the attitudes, ethos and values of an organisation. Answers to your questions about flexibility, commitment to training and encouragement to use your own ideas all give you clues to what that culture is.

You may have questions concerning such matters as accommodation or living costs in the area, availability of suitable housing, local schools, etc., if you would have to relocate to take up the job. It is not unreasonable to ask about these things, but don't take up too much time on these issues. This is very much the kind of information you can glean from other members of staff either before or after your interview in a more informal setting.

Nice and easy

A seemingly easy interview is not necessarily nice. One situation that can come as a bit of a surprise is the interview where you feel you haven't been asked much at all and haven't been given the inquisitorial grilling you anticipated and prepared for. After the initial relief a few minutes into the interview, you should start considering what is going on and whether there is anything you can or should do about it. There are several possible explanations for the interview taking this form.

The first and most pessimistic prognosis is that the interviewer has already switched off and so won't invest any energy in finding out more. Perhaps they have already seen a candidate who has impressed them so much that all your efforts are in vain. Maybe that rapport, that sparkle, simply isn't there. You can usually tell if this is the case, because the interview is short, you are asked few follow-up questions and you aren't encouraged to expand on your replies. More than this, your own gut feelings warn you that this is a lost cause.

There is a second and most optimistic possibility, namely that you have hit it off really well with the interviewer, you are that candidate who is going to render your competitors' efforts useless. Your future employer is already convinced that you are the ideal recruit and, aside from making sure there are no dreadful skeletons in your cupboard, they see no need to pursue the matter any further.

Delightful as this scenario is, do not allow yourself to bask in a smug state of certainty. Carry on putting a real effort into your performance – another sparkling candidate could be about to enter the room just as you leave it.

Unrelated to the two reasons above is the likelihood that the interviewer is simply not skilled in questioning: they may have had limited experience of conducting selection interviews and may be unaware of how to get the right information. You are less likely to encounter this situation if you are being interviewed by a large company or organisation where there is a human resource department and where managers are trained and experienced in all aspects of the recruitment process. You might encounter inexperienced interviewers with a small company, or if you are sent for a technical interview when you have been successful at your initial interview. You may be someone's first candidate or they may be jaded by years and years of recruitment interviewing.

The final option is the one where there is the greatest opportunity for you to take the initiative – the first is probably a lost cause and with the second you have very little to worry about. The reason that you need to take the initiative is that it is all very well feeling that you have come out of an interview having learned everything about the history of the company and the personal circumstances of your questioner, but if they have treated other candidates in the same way, how do they make their selection when they have seen every candidate?

Here are some possible questions or comments that you could make that begin to distinguish you from the crowd. You do need to ensure that you don't offend the interviewer, by cutting them off in mid flow, so wait for a pause, but be prepared to jump in quickly before they start up again.

(Q) **It sounds as if the company has had a really interesting history. Where do you see it going in the next year or two?**

(Q) **It sounds as if you really enjoy working here. Who would I be working with if you took me on?**

(A) Yes, your latest product range is impressive; the things I particularly like about it are …

(A) It is interesting that you say you much prefer working for a smaller set-up like this. I would really like to make the move to a smaller company where, whatever my specific responsibilities, I could feel far more involved and have a much greater understanding of everything we do and that is very much how you describe your role here.

(A) What you say about that recent project sounds really interesting. I really enjoyed the marketing project I did in the final year of my course because it took me out of university and gave me opportunities to meet people from the industry. It gave me a real basis for comparison when I started making my job applications and, although I didn't visit your company as part of my project, I really liked what I have found out and particularly all the useful information you have given me this morning.

brilliant tip

You can also grab the opportunity when asked 'Is there anything else you would like to ask me?' Turn the situation around with a reply such as one of the following:

A Well, I don't actually have any questions, as you have given me a great deal of useful information, but there are one or two points I would like to make, if I may, that highlight some aspects of my current work which are extremely relevant to the post I am applying for.

A Not exactly questions, but I would like to tell you a little bit about a project I undertook while I was a student which looked at how to develop better customer after-care for services like the one you provide.

Nightmare to avoid

One candidate took his quest for control to such an extent that he took to whispering the word 'me' whenever the interviewer used phrases such as 'the person we appoint' or 'the successful candidate'. His attempt to tap into the deeper levels of his interviewer's consciousness did no good whatsoever, since she assumed he was at best a little odd and at worst ... well, sinister would be an understatement.

brilliant tip

In a good interview, you, the candidate, should be speaking for about 80 per cent of the time. Again, it is one of those situations where you are rather in the hands of the interviewer. Trust your own

▶

communication skills, intuition and common sense to judge when it is acceptable to take control of a conversation and begin adding points of your own. If the interviewer hasn't given you a chance to shine, remember that he or she may have been interviewing all day, so take the initiative.

Gathering information – you in the hot seat

There is one kind of interview where you are very much in control – information-gathering interviews. On these occasions you set up the interview to find out more about a particular organisation or, more often, a particular type of work – quantity surveyor, retail buyer, occupational therapist or curator of meteorites (yes, there is such a job).

These information-gathering interviews are especially useful if you are at the point of making a career decision, be that on leaving school, university or college, or a change of direction somewhere along your career path.

You arrange the interview yourself, requesting someone to spend a little of their time talking to you about their work and what it involves. You can do this by writing or telephoning likely people or organisations or, if you are lucky, you may have friends or contacts within your selected profession who can help out with this.

brilliant tip

Researching information in this way can save you hours of online, telephone and paper research. Don't be afraid to try this – it is amazing how many people, even busy people, are happy to talk about their work.

You can also get the kinds of information, positive and negative, that you would never get from any other source; so long as you bear in mind that this information is necessarily subjective and coloured with your interviewee's own opinions and experience.

Nightmare to avoid

An applicant considering training in midwifery telephoned what she believed was her local hospital midwifery department to ask whether she could come in and talk about the work and perhaps help out a little bit in the department. She had actually got through to her local university library, where the chief librarian readily acceded to her request. It was only when she said she hoped she could witness a few births, perhaps including at least one Caesarean, that the penny dropped. If you are arranging to talk to someone about their work and your career, make sure you really do know to whom you are talking.

If you decide to organise some of these interviews for yourself you will find Chapter 3 helpful in planning your questions. Of course, your information-gathering won't be nearly as formal, but planned questions act as good prompts and give the impression that you value someone's time. It also helps you ensure that you really do get the sort of information that is going to be useful to you.

Here are some examples of questions that could help you get the discussion going. Remember not to ask any closed questions that leave someone with the option of simply saying 'yes' or 'no'.

Q **How long have you worked here?**

Q **What does your actual day-to-day work involve?**

Q **Could you describe a typical day or a typical week for me, if there is such a thing in this job?**

(Q) What do you most enjoy about working here?

(Q) What are the things that are most difficult to deal with in your job?

(Q) How typical do you think this firm/school/Civil Service department/agency is? Have you worked for any others?

(Q) How would you describe the management style here?

(Q) Would you recommend someone to enter this profession?

(Q) What do you think it takes to be really successful in this job?

(Q) What are the opportunities like for career progression either here or by moving to similar organisations?

(Q) What is the working atmosphere like here? Do you tend to socialise with colleagues outside working hours?

(Q) Is there much opportunity to get training? What sort of attitude is there to staff development?

(Q) What are the main issues that you feel this profession/company/business has to face over the next few years?

(Q) What significant changes have you seen since you started work in this industry/profession?

(Q) What do you expect to be the most significant changes that will come about in the next decade?

(Q) What would you advise someone in my position to do if I wish to gain more experience?

As well as becoming more well-informed by conducting such interviews, there is also a possibility that you can turn the situation to your advantage by making useful contacts who, even if they are not in a position to offer you employment there and then, are impressed enough to bear you in mind, or can put you in touch with contacts of their own, who may be able to offer you something. You can begin to build up a network within your chosen career, which will lead to future selection interviews, rather than information interviews.

Be pleasant, persistent and enthusiastic in your quest for this information. It really is worth the time and trouble.

Summary and reminders

Don't be caught unawares by suddenly having to ask rather than answer questions. The benefits of being able to ask questions are twofold – you can find out answers to things you really want to know and you can be sure that you are a thoughtful and confident applicant.

1   Prepare your questions in advance, but don't ask questions just for the sake of it.

2   Remind yourself of your main selling points, so that if nobody asks you about them you are prepared to grab opportunities to mention them.

3   Remember that these situations provide a wonderful chance for you to demonstrate your very good interpersonal skills.

CHAPTER 12

And finally

Learning from every interview, planning for future success and managing less typical interviews

Your interview is behind you and, unlike exams, you don't meet the rest of the candidates in the corridor saying they have revised the wrong bit or that they can't believe how easy it was. You are even spared the one person who declares that they have failed and the whole thing was a complete disaster, while you and everyone else in the class knows that they will get the top mark for the year.

You have the luxury of dealing with your reactions in private, but on most occasions you also have the anxiety of a wait of anything between a few hours and a few days. This is dependent on if and when they are seeing other candidates and also on whether other staff are involved in the decision – maybe human resources, finance or other line managers have a say.

Whatever the situation, don't let your performance in the closing minutes of the interview disintegrate through a sense of relief, optimism, gloom or exhaustion. Keep sparkling until the last handshake and the parting smile is over and the interview room door is closed firmly behind you.

Thoughtful interviewers will remember to tell you what the time-frame for their decision is likely to be and when and how successful candidates are to be informed, and whether or not they contact unsuccessful candidates too.

Q **When will you be able to let me know the result of this interview, please?**

Q **Do you usually telephone, e-mail or write to the successful candidate?**

(Let's hope they are not just going to send a text message – especially if you are not the successful candidate).

Q **Do you normally contact the candidates who have not been successful?**

Q **You do have my telephone number, mobile, etc., if you need to get in touch with me?**

Nightmare to avoid

One candidate was so desperate to know the result of his interview that he told the panel he was going on holiday for three weeks that evening, so could they possibly let him know now? He wasn't and they did. He hadn't got the job.

If you know that other candidates are being seen over the coming few days, you could write a letter after your interview, thanking your interviewer for their time, stating what interested you and confirming your enthusiasm for the job, and reminding them of your selling points. A letter such as this is unlikely to clinch a decision one way or the other, but it can do no harm and it may just put you back in their minds when they come to sum up all the candidates and review their notes.

Always thank your interviewer(s) before you leave, maintain your poise and breezy confidence and tell them you have found the interview interesting/very useful/enjoyable; it has confirmed and increased your enthusiasm for the post, the work, the organisation – whatever words you can find that sound neither too false nor too pleading, but which leave a positive impression as you depart.

There are two usual results to any job interview: either you get the job or you do not. There are others: you are the second choice and their first choice turns them down; they can't offer you anything now, but they will in the future if they can, etc.; but these constitute a minority of cases.

brilliant tip

If you are offered the job on the spot, it is best to accept it enthusiastically (unless of course you know you are definitely not interested). You need to appear decisive (especially if you have said you are a good decision maker), and to seem to dither really doesn't go down well. You may want to spend the evening thinking about it, talking it through with family members or friends, but if you seem indecisive at the interview you may miss the boat. One word of caution – don't give your acceptance in writing unless you really are sure you want the job.

Not being offered a job, particularly if it was one that you really wanted very much, is a disheartening experience, but you must not let disappointment taint your performance at future interviews. The following advice and suggestions on assessing your performance and planning for the future will help you gain and learn from each interview you attend.

If you are not offered the job, it is essential that you don't presume this was because you were a hopeless failure. Few of us have only one friend, dream of only one holiday destination, or feel tempted by only one dish on a menu, so why should only one candidate be suitable for a job?

Among the many potential reasons for not being offered a job after an interview are:

1 You were fine, but another candidate was better.

2 Perhaps you would have been the best person for the job, but interviews are always a subjective selection tool and they don't always lead to the selection of the most suitable person.

3 You and the interviewer simply didn't have a rapport.

4 It was a close-run thing between you and another candidate and, in the end, the selection boiled down to luck as much as to judgement.

5 Other candidates were better prepared, overall, for the interview and so more able to convey their suitability to the interviewer.

6 The selector(s) decided that, on this occasion, none of the applicants was suitable.

7 There were questions in the interview that you found difficult to answer.

8 Your overall interview performance was not brilliant – you just didn't have that sparkle on the day.

Many of the above reasons are beyond your control, but you are well placed to tackle the final two, examining how well prepared you were overall and asking yourself whether there were specific questions that you could have answered more effectively and with more panache if you had been better armed to face them.

It is hard when you first leave the interview because, though it is fresh in your mind, you are tired and whatever gut feelings you have about the result, you don't actually know whether or not you have been successful. Nevertheless, you must use this opportunity, when the experience is still fresh in your memory, to take a little time to sit down, reflect coolly on your performance and make sure that, if necessary, you can do better next time.

Sometimes kindly interviewers will provide feedback. This is really valuable, but it is by no means automatically available.

brilliant tip

Do make it clear that you can be flexible about when you get this feedback. They will want to speak to their favoured candidate first. Do express appreciation that they are prepared to give feedback to candidates.

After you have left the interview and at least allowed yourself a cup of tea or coffee, a bar of chocolate or whatever is your particular indulgence, review your interview critically:

- What were the names and positions of the person or people who interviewed you? You may be speaking to them again.
- What was the agreed arrangement for informing candidates of the outcome?
- Is there likely to be a follow-up interview, personality or aptitude test, or any other additional form of selection to build on this initial interview?
- Were there questions for which you were not well prepared? How would you prepare for these in the future?
- Were there questions that you answered well? What made these successful in your eyes and how can you transfer this success to your weaker topics?
- How great a part did your nerves play in your performance?

- Did you find out whether other opportunities are likely to arise with the organisation, even if you were not successful on this occasion?

- Were you able to get satisfactory answers to your own questions?

- What lasting impression do you think you made during your interview? Were you quiet and shy, or did you come across as friendly and confident?

- What was the most difficult question you had to answer?

- Did you take the opportunity to ensure that you got your key selling points across?

- Would you really have liked the job?

- Have you gained any new insight into the organisation, its work, your chosen career?

- Have you gained any new personal insight?

The point of going through these questions is not to encourage you into masochistic waves of self-doubt and gloom, nor indeed to confirm that all interviewers are mean and narrow-minded and just haven't seen you for the wonderful and capable person you really are. It is to ensure that you give an even better performance next time.

In a perfect world, we would be able to test out our interview techniques on employers who weren't really our first choice, so that these served as dress rehearsals for the ones we really care about. Providence is not always so generous, so you must treat every interview as if it really matters – after all, you can always turn the job down if the employer doesn't come up to scratch.

Having reviewed your performance using the above questions, make notes on these and draw up an action plan to enhance your future interview success:

- What research should I do next time and what resources can I use?

- For which questions do I need to work out better answers?

- Are there any aspects of my personal performance I need to improve on, e.g. being more assertive, trying to do more to combat my nerves?

The same time, but not the same place

While you are still most likely to be interviewed at the offices of a would-be employer, there are other possibilities. You may be invited to an interview in a more informal setting such as a hotel or a restaurant, and some employers use no premises at all – they interview you on the telephone or by videoconference.

Don't hang up

Telephone interviews are used either by large organisations that are recruiting several staff at the same time and can use the fairly brief telephone interview as a first stage of selection (most commonly after receipt of a CV or application form), or by companies recruiting staff whose work will necessitate them having a good telephone manner: telesales or call-centre work, for example.

brilliant tips

- Do prepare just as thoroughly and carefully as you would for any other interview.

- Do keep a list of the applications you have made close to your telephone, so that you don't get caught unawares.

- Do make sure you have set aside plenty of time.

- Do ensure that you have somewhere quiet to talk, so that you can concentrate.

▶

- Don't take the interview less seriously because you have not had to put on your smart clothes.
- Don't have other people hanging around who might distract you.

Really think about how you sound. On the telephone you can't rely on any of the non-verbal clues and cues you would normally give – your friendly smile, your firm handshake, the confident way in which you take your seat, or the way that you maintain good eye contact with your interviewer. You need to concentrate on putting feeling and enthusiasm into your tone of voice. Obviously you should use this in ordinary interviews too, but it is even more crucial when your voice is all the interviewer has to go on, apart from what is written on your CV.

brilliant tip

Improve your confidence on the telephone. Get a friend to help you with this exercise. Either telephone them or, if you are in the same room, sit back to back, so that they have no visual clues. Pick some entirely neutral words, for example numbers between one and twenty. Think of an emotion and say one of these neutral words, trying to convey that feeling of pleasure, irritation, enthusiasm, anger, etc., and see if the friend can label the emotions correctly. When talking to employers, stick to the pleasure and enthusiasm – the anger and irritation are only to help you develop your technique.

You may feel foolish, but you could also try calling your own answerphone and leaving a message just to hear how you sound. You should rehearse exactly what you are going to say at the start of the call, especially if you have been asked to telephone the employer – the impression you give as you introduce yourself is very important.

If you are initiating what could turn out to be a telephone interview, for example calling an employer to see if they have vacancies or just to ask to whom you should address your enquiries, you should still have a 'script' prepared. You may have called at an opportune moment when they are thinking of expanding or when a member of staff has just handed in their notice and your tentative enquiry could turn instantly into a selection interview.

Telephone interviews are quite difficult, but look on the bright side: at least you don't have to spend time and money on your interview wardrobe.

brilliant tip

Make a great impression by being confident of your selling points. Your 'script' should be rather like the essential points on your CV, though concentrating most particularly on what attracts you to the job/company/type of work, plus your relevant experience and qualities and your suitability and motivation. The hard part is fitting that into no more than 30 seconds, but it is worth doing and worth practising. Friends, who come in handy for so many aspects of interview preparation, can help out yet again.

Nightmare to avoid

Several telephone interviewees have been so determined to deliver their scripts that they have forgotten to check who is on the other end of the line. Your takeaway won't arrive any faster because the local restaurant now knows that you are a fully qualified and highly motivated environmental technologist, and the company's cleaning contractor may think you sound lovely but is unlikely to have the power to offer you employment.

An Oscar-winning performance

If you are a 3G mobile-phone enthusiast or you have made film clips to support your own website, then being interviewed via a video link may not be your worst nightmare, but most candidates, however techno-literate they may be, do find the idea daunting. Communications technology makes it easy for employers to use video interviews in some situations. They are used particularly by companies that are recruiting from overseas and where it is far less expensive to set up a video link than to send a panel of interviewers half way around the world.

Video interviews are far more like face-to-face interviews than telephone interviews, and you can't do them in your pyjamas or gym gear. The big mistake that interviewees make when faced with this form of selection is a tendency to look at what is happening on the screen rather than looking at the camera. Other than this, you simply have to tackle questions in exactly the same way as you would if you were in the same room as your interviewer(s).

One of the challenges of these interviews is that it can feel much more difficult to build up a rapport with your interviewer(s), even though they are probably giving off the same body language cues as in other situations. Try to be natural, speak clearly and put a bit of extra warmth into the whole thing if you can.

Eat, drink and be sensible

Most interviews take place in offices. They may occasionally resemble broom cupboards, but they are still official work premises. Some interviews take place in cafés, restaurants and bars, and these put candidates under considerable strain. You still want to get your selling points across and convince your interviewer that you are the right person for this job, while deciding how expensive a dish you dare order from the menu, what attitude to take to drinking alcohol and whether to tell your interviewer that they have parsley stuck between their teeth. On top of all this you don't want everyone to hear you explaining why you are the best investment manager, pensions analyst, financial futures dealer that ever walked the planet. (These examples have been used because this type of recruitment is not common for teachers, nurses or prison officers.) Keep your fingers crossed that none of the general public on this occasion includes any friends or colleagues.

The only advice that can really help here is sticking rigorously to all the common rules of courtesy that would apply when you are out eating or drinking.

Dos and don'ts

- Don't order the most expensive dish on the menu.
- Don't order anything that is likely to be messy and preoccupy you.
- Don't order anything if you don't know what it is.
- Do remember all your normal interview preparation.
- Do take a lead from your interviewers/hosts on drinks, number of courses to order, etc.
- Do avoid alcohol except in very small quantities.
- Do let your interviewer/host know in advance if you have special dietary requirements, e.g. vegetarian.
- Do try to enjoy your meal – not always easy!

Bear in mind that your 'interviewer', even if he or she has called it an informal meeting or a friendly chat, will still be working hard to assess whether you are the right person – whether you will fit in.

Even rarer than the 'informal' interview is the highly disconcerting situation where, for example, two candidates are interviewed at the same time – yes, in the same room – and have to compete to make the best impression. There are instances of ad agencies or PR consultants using this technique, but it is so uncommon that you need not lie awake at night wondering if it will happen to you. If it does, exactly the same rules apply as for any other interview – it is just that assertiveness and self-confidence will be two skills that are tested very directly.

It gets better all the time

Interview technique is, without question, something that you can improve with practice, and job interviews are something that we face throughout our working lives. Most interviews happen for the best reasons: you want a change, you want to move on, you want a challenge, or you have completed your education or training. Even those interviews that you have been obliged to go for, perhaps because of loss of a job or some other misfortune, are at least evidence that you are moving in the right direction – you are saying the right things on your written application.

Summary and reminders

When you have been for an interview – unless you have been successful, and you will be at some point – take the following steps.

1 Don't give yourself a hard time!
2 Be honest with yourself about your potential and your suitability for the next position you apply for.
3 Ensure that you have carried out any reasonable research about the work, the organisation and the specific post you have applied for.
4 Practise your interview technique with a friend, especially those questions that caught you out in any previous interviews.

5 It is difficult, but try to look forward to the interview and see it as something you will enjoy.

6 Be philosophical. If you don't get this next one, perhaps you would not have liked the job anyway, and there will always be other interviews.

Remember the advice of Henry Ford: that every failure is simply an opportunity to begin again, but this time with more intelligence.

Luck, providence, fate, whatever you wish to call it, always plays a role in interviews and job seeking, so may it be on your side and give you that little bit extra, in addition to all your own hard work and thorough preparation and sparkling performance.

Index of questions

Questions about education and qualifications

Questions about work experience and employment history

260 brilliant answers to tough interview questions

Q If we asked a colleague of yours to describe a fault
you have, what would they come up with?   54

Q How do you cope under pressure? This is a very
busy department you have applied to join.   54

Q How do you cope if a project you are working on
goes wrong?   55

Q Tell me how your experience to date makes you
suitable for this job.   57

Q What would you say is your greatest strength?   58

Q What is your time management like? How do you plan
your working week, for example?   59

Q How do you set about prioritising your workload?   59

Q What action do you take if you have members of staff
working for you who really don't get on with one another,
to the point where this is affecting other staff?   59

Q What sort of contribution do you make to a team or
work group?   60

Q What is the most difficult situation you have had to
deal with at work and how successful were you in dealing
with it?   60

Q What is the most satisfying aspect of your current
job?   60

Q Is there anything you don't like about your current
job?   61

Q Describe a situation where you have had to deal with
an angry customer/client/member of the public. How did
you cope and what was the outcome?   61

Questions to find out what you know about the organisation you are applying to

Questions about you – your achievements, your interests, your skills

Questions about career choice and career change

Questions about ambition, motivation and promotion

Questions that assess your ability to meet specific job requirements

Questions concerning weaknesses and perceived failures

Problem-solving or scenario questions

Current affairs questions

Questions concerning equal opportunities (some illegal)

Questions for you to ask

Questions to round things up